FREEDOM FROM THE PRESS

A Personal Story of Libel

SECOND EDITION

Roger Hall

MAHARATHA BOOKS
P.O. Box 638
Middleburg, Florida 32068
(904) 282-0103

Copyright © 1998 by Maharatha Books

Previous edition copyrighted in 1994

All rights reserved including the right of reproduction in whole or in part in any form.

Manufactured in the United States of America

Published by:

Maharatha Books
P.O. Box 638
Middleburg, Florida 32068
(904) 282-0103
maharatha@aol.com

ISBN 0-9643304-6-6

For Lester Hall
Who Taught Me When and How to Fight

For John Lennon
Who Led Me to Hope for a Day When There Are No Fights

Table of Contents

Preface	i
Introduction	v
Protection of Identity	x
In The Beginning	1
The War Begins	87
You Went To Prison For What?	127
Early Hope	136
Leaving Home	149
November Rain	166
The Day of Transition	177
Sold Out	208
Hunting Snakes	231
The Rockies Bring Me Home	273
Hunting Snakes In Peace	283
Suggestions to the High Court	298
Original Epilogue	313
Final Epilogue	317

Preface to the Second Edition

"The life of every man is a diary in which he means to write one story, and writes another; and his humblest hour is when he compares the volume as it is with what he vowed to make it."

- J.M. Barrie, <u>The Little Minister</u>, 1891

"If it suddenly ended tomorrow I could somehow adjust to the fall. Good times and riches and sons of a bitches -- I've seen more than I can recall."

-Jimmy Buffett, <u>Changes in Attitudes, Changes in Latitudes</u>, 1979

Freedom From The Press was originally written for, and distributed to the Supreme Court and Senate of the United States. In the four years since the first edition the book has been distributed hand to hand and marketed by word of mouth to an increasingly wide audience. If success can be measured by the kind words and letters of readers it has already enjoyed great success.

The second edition is the first commercial distribution of the book, and varies little from the original. In preparing the second edition it became apparent that predictions made four years before, i.e., the media (and self) demolition of President Clinton had come to pass.

Those who were instrumental in creation of the first edition have continued to be a source of ongoing and much appreciated support -- George and Ellen Ashby, Mitch and Liz Williams, Mike and Andy Marlatt, Ben and Carolyn Bryant. Special recognition is owed to Donna Plesser for the original editing. The cover has been changed, but the work of Ruth Hunter on the original will always be a key part of the ongoing story.

More than any others, the success the book has enjoyed is directly attributable to the roles Shelly, Elyssa, and Jeremy have played in my life. Were it not for them there would be no story to tell.

Following is the original preface from the first edition.

*****

I came from a lower middle class background and worked forty hours per week fronting a blast furnace during school to become the first person in the history of my family to earn a college degree. Education led to financial success, and financial success to pursuit of varied interests. Curiosity led to devastation.

Freedom From The Press ends the first part of my life. At age forty the time remaining in my life is an open issue. If it "suddenly ended tomorrow" there are a number of things I can be proud of -- my wife of twenty years chose to forego the money available to an M.D., Ph.D. female graduating first in her class in order to provide pediatric care to children who would have otherwise not had a doctor at all.

My children are beautiful and brilliant. The brilliance will be tempered by the example of their mother, and perhaps we will have created a legacy of medical care for the economically disadvantaged.

I can be proud of following the example of my father. He was a child of the depression in Salem, Arkansas. Born on the same day that would serve as the birth date for my hero John Lennon, and armed only with an inexplicable desire for something better he lied about his age to join the Navy and fight in the Pacific during World War II. Learning that there was more to life than ignorance and poverty he fought to escape, and did.

My father only has two gears. He is either the nicest man in the world who has literally given the shirt off his back to countless people down on their luck, or he is the worst possible nightmare of those who insist upon being cruel to those less able to fight. It has been said that I have only two gears as well.

My father taught me by example that the only reason you continue to fight sometimes is because there are no other viable options. There have been countless times during the battles recounted in this story when all I wanted to do was lie down and die. Each time something inside me refused to let that happen.

Whatever it is -- he helped put it there.

So the last thing to be proud of is that I am completely comfortable in the knowledge that I fought as hard as any human being could have fought against something that he truly believed was wrong.

INTRODUCTION

"A good name is rather to be chosen than great riches."
- Proverbs 22:1

"As it stands today, libel law is not worth saving. What we have is a system in which most claims are judicially foreclosed after costly litigation. It give plaintiffs delusions of large windfalls, defendants nightmares of intrusive and protracted litigation, and the public little assurance that the law favors truth over falsehood. If we can do no better, honesty and efficiency demand that we abolish the law of libel."

- Professor David A. Anderson[1]

"The Supreme Court created the law; it can change it. The problem with court reform is that it may never occur. There is no reason to believe that the Supreme Court is interested in modifying libel law. ."

- Professors John Soloski and Randall P. Bezanson[2]

I called your information line the other day. A really nice lady spent several minutes answering my questions and was kind

---

[1] David A. Anderson "Is Libel Law Worth Reforming?." University of Pennsylvania Law Review, December 1991.

[2] "Avenues for Reform", Reforming Libel Law, edited by John Soloski and Randall P. Bezanson, 1992.

enough to send me a pamphlet entitled "The Supreme Court of the United States." It says on page fourteen that your case load has increased steadily since 1945 to the point where you have about 6,500 cases on the docket per term. The pamphlet goes on to say that you prepare around 5,000 pages of opinions, dissenting opinions, and orders on the 115-130 cases that you actually choose for plenary review.

You should all say something nice to the person running the public information group. They're doing a good job.

Given this kind of work load I didn't want any of you to have to read very far to figure out the point of my book. If you want to see what libel law looks like to a plaintiff in the trenches this is for you. If you could care less, you can cut this exercise off at any time.

It is not a law book. I read the works of some extremely gifted professors of law in preparing it, but it is very much a personal story.

I don't know much about any of the nine of you, but hope that being a good lawyer is only a small part of what it takes to make it to the Supreme Court. I especially hope that having an open mind is part of the package as well -- open to the extent that a self-published book arriving in the mail from some unknown guy in Baja Georgia might be able to change your mind.

My objective is simple. I want you to make the law fair

again. Too often we see the pendulum swing from side to side on complex issues, never quite managing to stop in the middle. From what I have read I would most likely have voted with the majority in <u>New York Times v. Sullivan</u> in 1964. If at that time libel law was so biased in favor of plaintiffs that it threatened to silence the voice of opposition to segregation and oppression it most certainly needed revision. It is my sincere hope that libel law never becomes so restrictive that a free and <u>responsible</u> press fear expression of any position or opinion. That would make the creation of books like this one impossible.

    The book is written for the nine of you because I firmly and sincerely believe that you are the only ones that can change it. Legislators cannot change it because they cannot challenge the press -- to do so would mean their own destruction politically. The executive branch cannot do it for the same reason. Our information driven society has reached a point where the media literally has the power of selection in matters of election. Whether this is good or bad is not my concern. My concern is only the quality of the information used in exercise of the power.

    I do not harbor any resentment or hatred of the press. To the contrary each of my days is filled with reading -- often the output of the media. There are some incredibly gifted and ethical journalists in each branch of media. Different parts of <u>Freedom From The Press</u> were written at different times. Some of those times were filled with depression, resentment, and hatred. Please try to overlook the emotion of those periods should you choose to proceed, and remember that by the time you reach my specific suggestions to you in Chapter Twelve the mood will be that of this introduction.

Maybe this book will change your mind. Maybe it will never get past the filtering system for unsolicited mail that must surely exist for each of you. Either way I will have fulfilled my obligation and can go on with my life.

I should be dead. Really. The explanation of why and why not are in the first chapter. With my pardon came a burden of responsibility. Shortly after the events of the first chapter I took my children to a small park in a Jewish neighborhood near my home in Houston. As they scrambled to the toys I sat down at a picnic table to read a book on how to write a book. I have been seated at a number of picnic tables in my life, and do not recall many of them having brass plates with inscribed messages. This one did, and this is what it said:

"The Lord will see you through in this important work."

Any decisions as to the creative force or importance of this work are entirely yours. All I know is that I had no choice but to write it, it took three years of my life to do so, and as soon as it is mailed to you I can be done with it.

Thank you for your consideration, and may each of you

have long, happy, and productive careers as members of the Supreme Court.

Protection of Identity

This is a work dedicated to the reform of libel law in the United States. Therefore, it would be hypocrisy of the worst kind if I were to be guilty of libel in the effort.

Eight people will be directly or indirectly accused of heinous behavior in *Freedom From The Press*. I believe one of them to be guilty of committing multiple felonies in pursuit of wealth and power. At least two of the others have engaged in criminal conspiracy with this one.

Each of the eight have been assigned fictitious names. It is my belief that a "reasonable man" would not conduct the research necessary to tie the characters of my work to living persons. Such effort is not required to understand this text nor would the successful completion of detective activity affect the real objective of this text -- identification and reform of cruel and unusual law.

Should anyone choose to proceed with an attempt at identification they should not expect any support from either myself or the Department of Justice, which I understand to remain silent regarding ongoing investigations. Therefore, any implication of individuals would be made on a purely speculative basis without the accused having had the right to trial in the case of criminal behavior or rebuttal with regard to lesser charges. Anyone making public accusations prior to appropriate confirmation of guilt would, in my mind, be guilty of defamation.

I am convinced that all claims and anecdotes herein are true. But as Emily Dickinson said:

"The truth must dazzle gradually / Or every man be blind."

* * * * *

Six of the eight characters have been assigned the names of snakes. The easy thing to do is assume that such an assignment is intended to be trite and derogatory. That would be an assumption made by one who had never personally studied and done battle with snakes. Virtually all snakes, including venomous ones are harmless if left alone. It is only when we invade territory they believe to be their own that snakes begin to pose a threat -- and even then the vast majority will quickly flee if given the opportunity. Snakes serve a variety of valuable functions in nature. Rampant indiscriminate killing or harassment of any species would be irrational and imprudent.

Selection of a particular snake to represent a character was based upon my personal experience with that variety of snake. With all apologies to Roger Tory Peterson and other true biologists my behavioral classification may occasionally prove to be imprecise as regards the snake. However, the association of all referenced behavioral tendencies of snakes with human beings of similar character in this story has been made with great confidence.

*****

The six reptilian stand-ins and their two companion creatures are characterized below. Capitalization is used to indicate substitution for proper names.

Coachwhip

A relatively rare and reclusive snake preferring the dryer regions of Northern Florida. The Coachwhip will charge a human if challenged, but prefers to simply be left alone. Although not venomous the coachwhip poses a substantial threat to humans by virtue of its quickness, incredibly sharp teeth, and tendency to hold on rather than release after biting. The literature is ripe with stories of seeing four to seven foot Coachwhips flying through the air hanging on to large birds who have been the victim of attack.

My only personal experience with the Coachwhip came while observing one who had crossed my path on a deserted country road. After several minutes of allowing me to view him the snake suddenly charged from a distance of about ten yards. Barefoot and without a snake stick I was forced to fire one round from a Walther PPK .380 into him six inches behind his head. The shot nearly dissected the snake's seven foot long body but it took more than an hour to finally die. Setting a new standard for resiliency and aggressiveness he managed to push his dangling head out of the bucket in my front floorboard on the way home and try to bite my foot resting on the accelerator.

Cobra

The Cobra is sleek, cunning, and its lethality is the substance of legend. It has been used to symbolize insidious evil since the beginning of history.

Only a fool would hunt the Cobra for sport. However, once a human is confronted his options are to overcome incredible odds to defeat the viper or die. Left alone the Cobra will feed on a variety of living things and grow to a length of nineteen feet. Fortunately the Cobra is normally only seen in captivity.

Hog-Nose

The Hognose is all Hollywood. It is also known as the "bluffing adder" because of the tendency to flatten neck and head into a hood when confronted -- pretending to be the old world nemesis of man.

Not only does the Hog-nose lack venom, it does not even bite when striking. Hognose snakes rarely reach lengths of more than forty-two inches.

A good Hog-nose show will scare the hell out of most people, but snakehunters are only amused.

Diamondback

The Florida Diamondback is the largest of North American rattlesnakes. Experienced hunters around Jacksonville have many skins in excess of twelve feet although most books reference a maximum length of nine to ten feet. Diamondbacks have also been described as the heaviest poisonous snakes in the world. Although certainly not the longest they are the toughest and most muscular.

Some authors call the Diamondback the most dangerous of American snakes. My guess is that these people have never jumped barefooted into two feet of water intending to retrieve a dead Cottonmouth that has just been blown off a branch -- only to discover that it is still pretty healthy. The Diamondback is nonetheless, as can bediscovered in chapter eleven, a deceptive and formidable foe.

Pigmy

The Pigmy has a Napoleon complex. Its venom is similar to the Diamondback but short fangs and small supplies of venom make it more of a pain in the ass than a health threat. There are no documented deaths resulting from Pigmy nibbles.

Most hunters agree that the Pigmy does win the prize for the worst attitude. They are easily provoked and will strike repeatedly if afforded the opportunity. From my experience the pigmy is happiest when hiding in woodpiles waiting to hurt curious children or pets.

Cottonmouth

Call them Cottonmouth or Moccasin, head or foot they're a problem. You can never trust a Cottonmouth, but it is hard not to develop a respect for them. Even in areas where they are prevalent it is hard to get close enough to kill one. Your best bet is to find one sunning in the hot afternoon sun after a big meal. I don't remember skinning one that didn't have a recently ingested fish or frog in the digestive system. They flail violently in the coiled rope of a snakestick. The toughest of them take ten to fifteen minutes to die when choked by hand.

My favorite Cottonmouth story regards one my son found on the path between the river and our house. Taking no chances with one so close to home I cut him in half with a blow so violent that the handle of my scythe shattered. The front half of the snake charged my bare feet. I cut the front half in half. The snake could no longer charge, but looked at me with fangs extended and bit the air repeatedly. The quarter snake was still biting half an hour later. Cottonmouths come from the Samurai school of warfare -- for which they are to be respected.

Most people fail to realize how beautifully colored cottonmouths are as children and adolescents. They are characterized by two shades of copper that appear to be fiery orange and red-orange when swimming in sunlight -- terminated by a greenish yellow tail. As they grow older they lose their color -- often becoming nearly black -- a condition that serves to accentuate the white inside of the mouth as it is revealed during displays of aggression.

My fighter pilot neighbor granted me the nickname of "Rambo" after searching around in four feet of water with my bare hands for a moccasin he had shot swimming off his dock. In a community of S.E.A.L.s and fighter pilots it is a good nickname to have, but the truth is that if you take away guns, knives, throwing axes, Ninja stars, and snakesticks your average human would not fare well against a seven foot Cottonmouth. They are a worthy and fascinating opponent.

Maggot

The Maggot is, of course, not a snake at all neither is it particularly dangerous unless you happen to lie down in a big pile of them -- which would seem to me a foolish thing to do. Like many functionaries in modern society the Maggot creates nothing of value and survives on the waste or unprotected assets of productive creatures.

Scorpion

One would not expect to find a great number of astrology buffs on the High Court, but in case someone has a closet interest you might be interested in knowing that Scorpio has the greatest power for good and the greatest power for evil in the Zodiac. The capacities are in equal measure and purely a matter of personal choice. I have never encountered on in the wild.

In The Beginning

At the time of editing it had been two years since "Roger's Story" was written. It was done at a time when I was suffering from professionally diagnosed exogenous clinical depression, and usually only a few lines at a time. How it came to be completed under these conditions is a mystery to me, but it is nonetheless the best explanation available of the bizarre series of events that turned my life upside down.

A few factual issues will be expanded and clarified later in the book, especially those concerning my comments about the character to be known as Cobra. During the time this work was in process, my attorney had made it clear that any negative referral to Cobra would be at least dangerous to the legal effort, and quite possibly to my family as well.

The day that I was finally emotionally prepared to review "Roger's Story" for inclusion in this book a talented young voice for his generation, Nirvana's Kurt Cobain, killed himself. Kurt had a head full of heroin, but lots of people run around for years with heads full of heroin without killing themselves. Mainly, Kurt was depressed.

Reading this story for the first time in two years left me

deeply concerned about the odd nature of suicidal thought. Often suicide attempts are shallow threats made in hope of receiving attention. From my experience, the real danger comes when the decision to end your life is as logical and peaceful as picking up the morning paper. To the extent that you may have been personally touched by suicide I hope that the tranquil nature of the final moments give you some comfort. If you think that you might be touched, I hope that the story alerts you to the danger of silence.

Roger's Story

But, as they watched, unbelievably the side of the hill seemed to open: a narrow, dark corridor appeared and the piper, followed by the children, disappeared inside. When all were gone, the great door shut fast and there was silence.
Only one child was left. A lame boy who hadn't been able to keep up with his friends.
As you may imagine, the town of Hamelin was a very sad and quiet place for many years afterwards, and the story of that awful day was carved on a stone by the Koppelberg Hill -- as a reminder to all . . .

Retold by Kay Brown from the poem by Robert Browning, "The Pied Piper of Hamelin"

Probably the best way to begin this story is with a brief description of who I am.

I'm nobody.

Thank God I'm lame.

It wasn't too long ago, or maybe it was a really long time ago, that I was valedictorian of my high school, honor student at two universities, star of the 1972 NAIA National Championship football game, top producer in the history of the nation's top privately held commercial real estate firm, founder of three major social programs, expert witness before the Senate of the

United States in hearings on improving the country's child care system, one of Five Outstanding Young Houstonians (George Bush and Denton Cooley were prior recipients of the award), granted several commendations from groups like the United States Department of Justice, and even financially successful if you consider $350,000 a year while devoting only twenty hours a week to your job successful. Money never was the real payoff for me in what many would probably call financial success. The fun part was paying for formula for babies with AIDS, picking up the airfare for the families of heart transplant patients to come to Houston when they couldn't afford it themselves, buying an infant warmer for the family center at the hospital where my kids were born, and basically being able to afford to do all the kinds of things that many people would do if they had access to the money. Don't even consider thinking that I am trying to pass myself off as an innocent angel. Absolutely nothing could be farther from the truth. I am, and take great pride in being, a temperamental renegade with very few friends outside my own family. In all honesty, the public service activity satisfied my only need for social interaction, since hanging out and spending money with a bunch of BMW-driving, Rolex-wearing yuppies made me sick. I preferred to be with nuns. In my opinion, the old Catholic ladies who took care of the AIDS babies were kind of renegades themselves and infinitely more fun to be around than those in my profession.

Ten years of quiet public service and hundreds of

thousands of dollars in time and donations never warranted a paragraph in the local papers.

But on Sunday, September 1, 1991, the *Houston Chronicle,* Texas' largest newspaper, ran excerpts from my deposition in the case of *Wyatt v. Sakowitz* with "A Cult of the Wealthy" as the front page banner headline, along with a picture of me running at Memorial Park in Houston. The author didn't bother, or forgot, to mention that most of the information in my deposition was taken from interviews with former members of the cult, such as co-founder John Andreadis and high fashion model Susan Bearden. In the deposition, it is clear that I had never taken psychedelic drugs, kissed any boys except my son and my dad, and I did not have any meaningful interaction with any of the inner circle except Douglas Wyatt, who was my lawyer and running partner. But the caption by my picture read something like "Friend and Rich Lawyer Have Weird Sex With Drug Taking Aliens From Outer Space." The day the article came out, Cobra called me and let me know that the real motivation of the Chronicle was to publicly embarrass Oscar Wyatt, stepfather of Douglas, generally because they hated him and specifically because he had won a libel suit against them. I had become a rowboat wedged between the Titanic and the iceberg.

Lurking behind a facade that I now believe could have only been learned at the feet of one of the two greatest masters of evil deception of the twentieth century, Frederick von Mierers,

Douglas Wyatt took me through a meticulous and bizarre process that was designed to ultimately get me to become a homosexual, leave my family, become a member of his cult, and move to their armed compound in North Carolina. Doug's mistake was in the selection of his victim, failing to understand that street kids can have their own agenda when interacting with the rich and famous. But the point of my story is the process of recruitment used by Doug Wyatt and his master. . . .both brilliant students of Adolph Hitler.

To start, it is unlikely that many people would have wanted to jump right into Doug's cult, known as "The Eternal Values," if they told you up front that you needed to abandon your wife and kids, give them all your money, eat some magic mushrooms, and get used to the idea that getting humped in the butt by a space alien with AIDS is all part of getting right with God. The very nature of the process that Doug Wyatt stalked me with demanded stealth and patience. Doug had other deathly serious reasons for a low-profile recruitment as well. Even the faintest hint in the Houston business community or his international social circle that he was gay would have destroyed him. Susan Bearden, the Ford Agency model who pretended to be his fiance for two years in the interest of presenting a heterosexual cover, told me in my first conversation with her that his stepfather Oscar had already disowned a blood son for being a homosexual. There are a lot of gay people who think it is more important to be honest with themselves than to please others, but most of them don't have parents who are not particularly healthy (as Doug often mentioned) with a net worth of $400 million or so. Unknown to his parents, Doug had the additional problem of responsibility for financial support of a large group of bisexual friends. Given his repressed sexuality, the opportunity for him to find a guilt-free outlet at the Manhattan apartments leased by Eternal Values was, in itself, probably enough to guarantee his involvement.

But how did they go about getting money from others, including me and Doug Wyatt's mother, who were not homosexual and generally opposed to every central teaching of his cult?

My first interaction with Doug Wyatt resulted from the fact that his law firm and my wholly owned real estate company were both members of a pool that shared four seats at courtside for the Houston Rockets basketball games since none of us in the pool wanted to pay $100 a seat for every game of the season. The seats were ideal client entertainment, especially since I never had more than five clients at any given time. DHL Worldwide Express, Coca-Cola, and a handful of other companies were critically important to my business, and their representatives often enjoyed seeing a basketball game at floor level. When the tickets were distributed before the season, we applied a complex formula for allocation of tickets to pool members based on won-loss records of the opponents, years in the pool, etc. Then for the rest of the year there was a never-ending exchange of phone calls and trades resulting from the real wants and needs of the members. Each of us had a list of names and phone numbers of the pool members, as well as a breakdown of where the tickets had gone on initial distribution. In a sense, the downfall of my professional life is directly attributable to the fact that the regional manager for DHL Worldwide Express was a big fan of the Utah Jazz, especially Karl "The Mailman" Malone. I was in great shape for a trade when he called me for tickets, since it was early in the season and I still had Lakers, Pistons, and Celtics games in my drawer. All I had to do was call 877-6355 and ask for a guy named Wyatt.

* * * * *

"I'm Doug Wyatt."

He was thirty minutes late for lunch, and I was in the middle of selling some orange groves for Coca-Cola that, thanks to a wildcat freeze and the explosive growth of Orlando, Florida, had become highly sought commercial property. I didn't have time to wait for a yuppie lawyer, no matter how much the guy at DHL wanted to see the Mailman.

"Thanks for coming. It's really good of you to bail me out on this. . . ."

"No problem. I'm really sorry for being late. My dad called as I was leaving."

I honestly had no clue whatsoever that he was referring to

Oscar Wyatt, self-made multimillionaire, Chairman of Coastal Corporation, one of the most profitable major oil and gas companies, and, by his own admission, one of the toughest businessmen in America. Later it would become clear to me that when dad called, the world could wait. But at the moment, this lunch Doug had requested to exchange the tickets was becoming a major waste of my time.

"I'm really short on time. You care if we just eat the buffet?"

"That's great. I'm running behind too."

The lunch buffet at City Lights, the restaurant on top of Stouffer's Presidente hotel in Greenway Plaza is one of the best kept secrets in Houston. For ten bucks, you get a gourmet salad bar, fresh vegetables, prime rib or brisket, and the best selection of desserts in town. It was my favorite place for a business lunch, because it left you in total control of your pace. You could push through in fifteen minutes or take as long as you wanted, drinking and talking with a client while looking across the Southwest Freeway at the downtown Houston skyline. As was usually the case on days when I had run my scheduled six miles in the morning, lunch was an experience in volume. I came back to the table with shrimp salad, prime rib, broiled potatoes, fresh bread, and two pieces of cheesecake. Doug had a small plate with about five raw spinach leaves and a glass of water.

"Aren't you hungry?"

"My mother is having a dinner party tonight, and I'll eat a

lot then."

Doug reached in the vest pocket of his suit, which didn't look like it had come off the rack at Sears, and extracted a plastic package with a large handful of capsules and tablets. He proceeded to swallow pills for about three minutes. I was afraid the poor son of a bitch had terminal cancer or something. It would be a long time before I knew why colon cleansers were so important to him.

As I inhaled lunch and watched him swallow a week's production of Wyeth labs, I took my first real look at him. Doug was six feet four, slim, and one of those Jewish guys that looked like an Italian guy. Although I had gotten through college fronting a blast furnace at night and scraping pigeon shit out of cages in a psychology laboratory before school in the morning, life had been quite good in Houston, so I knew a bit about custom-made suits. Doug's hand-tailored, charcoal gray suit was worthy of Roberto Goizueta, the dapper Chairman of Coca-Cola, who I had often seen while doing business in Atlanta. This was one successful lawyer.

"So what kind of law do you do?"

"Mostly litigation. We do a lot of take or pay cases for Coastal."

"Are they your biggest client?"

"Yeah. They get sued quite a bit."

We ran through the usual introductory bit of business gibberish inherent in any new meeting with an unknown entity.

Where did you go to school, how many kids do you have, what does your wife do, etc. From my experience, it was not particularly unusual that a good-looking, well-to-do guy like Doug would be single, even though he appeared to be in his early thirties. My best friend, a Jewish orthopedic surgeon, refuses to even consider getting married until he has had sex with at least thirty percent of the women on the East Coast. Could be any time now. Doug was as polished and aggressive a businessman as I had met.

The conversation took an unusual turn when we got to the area of hobbies. We were both runners. He had run track at St. Johns, which I knew was the school for the extremely wealthy kids in Houston, and he had to keep running as fitness was a critical part of education when he went to college at Washington and Lee.

My favorite topic was one that most business people avoid like African bees -- religion. I had clients and friends ranging from the head of the Anti-Defamation League in Texas to an elder in a fundamentalist Baptist church. I was always curious about the spiritual orientation of anyone, and particularly the wealthy and successful. To the man, the most successful people that I had met or worked with were deeply influenced by their faith in God, if you could ever get them to admit it.

When I asked Doug where he went to church, he came alive.

"Why do you ask?"

"Nothing personal. I've been involved in everything from preaching for the Church of Christ in junior high to going to Fairfield, Iowa, to hear Maharashi Mahesh Yogi announce the Dawn of the Age of Enlightenment."

He paused for just long enough to assess the sincerity of my answer, and said:

"I'm pursing a path that some might refer to as metaphysical. Not in the sense of a Shirley MacLaine -- she's such a bitch."

"Have you read her reincarnation stuff?"

"No. When I had dinner with her in Los Angeles it was obvious that she was just another publicity hungry cunt interested in getting attention."

Either this guy was a pathological liar, or he had a personal relationship with my hero Jack Nicholson's date in "Terms of Endearment." Now I was awake, too.

"You had dinner with Shirley MacLaine?"

"She's a friend of my mother. Mom enjoys her show business friends, especially Charlton Heston."

I was seriously outclassed, and out of time. I had already thrown my American Express Platinum card on the bill, in a faint-hearted attempt at financial equality, and as the waitress took it away, said:

"Thanks again, Doug. You saved my ass on the Utah game."

"Anytime. I'm going to have a courier bring you some

tapes this afternoon."

Two hours later, and just about the time my partner had finished explaining to me that I had just made friends with one of the richest guys in Texas, the package, which I had dismissed as an idle promise, arrived. The titles alone were alluring for any student of religion or philosophy, "From Creation to the Fall of Man", "The Beyond: Life Between Death and Birth", "Karma and Destiny", "Jnana Yoga", and even a three-volume dissertation on "The Dark Forces" that currently control the Earth. I was particularly intrigued by the title "Space People".

On the way home from the office, I couldn't wait to pop "Karma and Destiny" in the tape player to hear about this religion of the upper class.

The voice of Frederick von Mierers is evidence of the fact that he is not from around here. I mean psychologically, although his cult members literally mean from another solar system. After a day of my usual verbal tirades against the evil landlords of the Northeast, and the accompanying stress and anger, within three minutes of the time he began to speak I was totally calm and at peace. The deep confidence and strength in the voice of this man from New York was simultaneously stimulating and hypnotic.

At the time of this first introduction to the philosophy of Frederick von Mierers and Eternal Values, I was deeply involved in an effort to raise money for pediatric AIDS patients in Houston. In 1988, Houston was not a good place for a businessman to be involved in any activity related to AIDS, for the predominant attitude at the top of the business community could be summed up as "the faggots got a message from God if you ask me." But even the most calloused and cold of the oil field service industry would be liable to come up with a few bucks if you did a good job explaining that children got it either from their mother perinatally or from a tainted blood transfusion. My anti-drug program was becoming a huge success, and the same cadre of business leaders that supported it were targets for money for the little people who would die a horrible death before they were seven through absolutely no fault of their own.

My unresolved emotional issue was that I would go to the Children's Home, which was the only real source of relief for the kids in Harris County at the time, play with and hold Brittany, my two-year-old buddy, then try to figure out how a loving God could let a beautiful little black girl be born to a junkie mother, infected before birth with a killer virus, and then abandoned naked on the floor of a downtown warehouse on a cold January morning.

In the first tape I ever heard from von Mierers, he explained the Hindu answer to my question in a parable related to the philosophy of Karma and reincarnation. The message of his tape was that the results of our actions always come back to us in the same form that we send them out. How many times have you heard a Christian or Jew say that "what goes around comes around"? The new twist, and one of the most intriguing thoughts ever presented to me, was that death does not allow us to escape any outstanding negative karma. We simply reincarnate in an appropriate body and location to allow us to deal with the remainder of our rebounding actions. We continue to reincarnate, learn, and suffer until we understand enough of the positive light of God's nature to allow us to progress on to a higher plane of consciousness, i.e., become closer to God in a real sense. In particular, he gave the example of a mulatto child born blind into a family that cared little for it. On the surface, it would appear that this were the callous action of a vengeful and hateful God. If, however, we understood that in its last reincarnation this child had been an evil slave trader that put out the eyes of runaway slave children with a hot poker, we would understand how this condition was necessary for the blind child to progress beyond the terrible debt that it had incurred. Von Mierers even made it clear that we, as more fortunate souls, were to shower these suffering souls who were paying their debt to the universe with love and help. Even today, I find this explanation as fascinating as any for the pain all around us on this planet.

Over the course of the next week, I listened to all the tapes. Again and again, the meticulous weave of Christianity, Judaism, Hinduism, and Islam into an intellectual fabric designed to explain the entire world before me was a source of peace and insight.

It would be nearly two years later, during the word by word analysis of the Eternal Values tapes in preparation for my deposition in the case of *Wyatt v. Sakowitz*, that I would first hear the buried comments and themes of hate and brainwashing in these auditory masterpieces. Even the revelation that the Jews in Nazi Germany got what they deserved is buried in an otherwise beautiful dissertation on the Christian philosophy of "Do unto others as you would have them do unto you," and was camouflaged in the teaching that they had to be tortured because they had been the Christians in the Inquisition that had tortured Jews and that they had reincarnated en masse that they might receive the same treatment at the hands of Adolph Hitler.

I had to replay the section five times in order to be able to make myself believe that he had really said that. It was my first exposure to professional brainwashing.

* * * * *

My relationship with Doug Wyatt and his new age friends began as a war over money.

Commercial real estate brokerage is a tough business. In general, as the dollars get bigger, the people get meaner, and in my business the numbers were pretty big. It was common for commissions to exceed $100,000, and some were in excess of $1,000,000. Major real estate deals are always difficult, and many of the ones that I worked on took years to complete. One of the hardest and longest was a cargo facility at Los Angeles International Airport (LAX) for DHL Worldwide Express, one of my first big exclusive clients. Working with an airport authority to do anything is like pushing a semi-solid cow pile up a flight of stairs, especially when the bureaucracy is as big and stagnant as the Los Angeles Department of Airports. We first began trying to get a site in the Imperial Cargo Complex at LAX for DHL in 1982. The deal finally got done in 1990. In what I believe is the key to any government real estate deal, it was necessary to find someone inside the bureaucracy who had some stroke and needed a favor.

Through a developer I had worked with in the past, we were introduced to one of the principals of a start up company that was going to specialize in the development of airport facilities. They had an experienced financial guy, a former operations executive of Braniff airlines, and most importantly, a close friend in the top of the bureaucracy in Los Angeles. Since timing is everything, it was really interesting for us on the DHL side of the deal to know that the former Braniff executive was on the selection committee for the hiring of a new Director of Airports for the City of Dallas. The guy in L.A. we had to deal with wanted the Dallas job in the worst way. Suddenly our phone calls were returned, approvals came quickly, and miraculously the deal came together right before the L.A. official moved to his new home in Dallas.

After eight years, the commission of $500,000 was not

looking as big as it once had, but it was still a considerable amount of money. Having spent most of my career working for slow but honest companies like Coca-Cola, it never occurred to me that we would get burned on a deal of this magnitude. In fact, over the course of ten years, I had billed over $50 million in commissions of different types and never had any trouble on any of them. However, when I called the financial man with the developer about funding and therefore the commission payment, he told me on the phone:

"Fuck you. If you want it, you can sue me."

He had a big time Napoleon complex, and I sincerely thought he was joking, or at worst making it known that he was finally an important man. A few more minutes of conversation made it clear that he was quite serious about keeping the $500,000 for himself.

Thinking this to be an odd attitude for a man who could directly attribute his first major deal and the subsequent successful start up of his company to a transaction that had been put together by me, I began to think about lawyers. Having never sued anyone before, I had no experience with litigators. It quickly occurred to me that it might be a good time to do some business with Doug Wyatt.

* * * * *

Looper, Reed, Ewing & McGraw was housed,

appropriately it would turn out, on the seventeenth floor of Coastal Tower in Houston's Greenway Plaza. The thirty-story, silver, reflective-glass, rectangular structure is one of a set of twin buildings, built during Houston's oil boom when maximization of floor size was infinitely more important than architectural quality. The Summit sports complex, where the Houston Rockets play their games, is adjacent to the buildings, and the towers gave rise to the nickname of the "Twin Towers" for Ralph Sampson and Hakeem Olajuwon when they were together on the Rockets.

Looper, Reed was a relatively small firm of twenty attorneys, and their office space was surrounded above, below, and even across the hall by sections of Oscar Wyatt's Coastal Corporation. Ostentatious finish is always a key component for a successful law firm, and they had spent as much money on the double entry doors to their suite as the gross national product for most Third World countries. Once inside, it was apparent that Brooks Brothers and Houston's Cosmetic Surgery Associates had just come off good quarters financially. It did not appear that anyone in the office was over forty, and most were under thirty. Especially prominent was the young receptionist, who was roughly a 40DD and quite fond of low-cut business attire. She was, I would learn later, methodically destroying the marriage of one of the managing partners.

As I was led to Doug's office, we went past the usual array of Martindell-Hubble directories, volumes of statutes, and other thick legal volumes that are seldom if ever opened but nevertheless provide the critical illusion of scholarliness for a law firm. Looking in the doors as we walked, the offices of the all-male attorney force were nothing extraordinary, comprised of tasteless, conservative office furnishings and huge mounds of paper on top of the desks. When we came to Doug's office, it was quite another matter. He was seated behind the largest Italian marble desk I had ever seen. Each of the walls were covered by beautiful works of art. Even his plants were exotic, rather than the usual philodendrons and fig trees. Hidden behind his leather sofa on one side of the room and by sculpture on the other were gently humming machines, which he told me were air purifiers and negative ion generators.

As we began to discuss my case, a phone, obscured by one of the plants, started to ring.

"That's dad."

Doug quickly excused himself and went to pick up the phone. They talked for several minutes, and it became apparent to me that Doug was reading off a list of state and county judges. It was not clear to me why until he said:

"I'm telling, you, Dad, these judges remember their contributors. We need to take it seriously."

It was my first up close and personal exposure to the harsh reality of justice in Texas, where the judiciary is elected rather than appointed on the basis of merit. I was hearing a prominent attorney tell his stepfather, the chairman of a major company, which coffers to fill for the greatest future return. He seemed to notice that I was listening, and the volume of his voice dwindled to the point where I could not hear the rest of the conversation. Before he returned a few minutes later, the first in a series of thoughts came to me that I would later regret. Here I was, in the palatial office of a well connected, influential attorney who had no qualms at all about suggesting that equal justice under the law had a price in Texas, and his firm had no problem in picking up the tab. As far as I was concerned, if that was the way the game had to be played to keep from getting screwed by my enemy, so be it.

When he returned, we finished our discussion of the facts of the case and agreed to meet again after Doug had time to read all the documents. Then the first question in the web arrived:

"What did you think of those tapes?"

"I'll tell you the truth, Doug, it is the most interesting explanation of God and his role in this world that I have ever heard."

"Great! Here, I've got one more set for you."

He went to the leather sofa, picked up a brown mail pouch, and pulled out a cellophane covered line of cassette tapes.

"And to think that I used to have drugs delivered in these things. Here you go."

Most lawyers would rather die than tell you their correct shoe size, and this guy was telling me that he was an old stoner in our first business meeting. My infatuation with drugs had been gone for several years, and some of the events from that era of my life had driven me to create a Drug Free Business Initiative that was becoming a major force for demand reduction in Houston. At least he was telling me that he "used to" get shipments. Houston was still a place where conservatism ruled, and admission to illegal drug use, even in the past, was a risky proposition that I had no interest in touching.

"Let me pay you for these things, Doug."

"Not a chance. It's a pleasure to meet someone who appreciates them."

He walked me back down the hallway, through the visually stimulating reception area, and out into the elevator lobby. We talked for a few minutes and agreed that we could talk about the lawsuit while running on the three-mile track around Memorial Park as well as anywhere.

"So your dad is right upstairs?"

I had not told him yet that his stepfather was one of my heroes, being rich, self-made, and widely disliked by the well respected men of a cutthroat community. He was even prominent in my favorite new book, *The Predator's Ball*, about Mike Milken and the corporate raiders.

"No. He's down on seven."

"Since when does the chairman of a major company reside anywhere except the top floor in the corner with the best view?"

"Since he found out that the ladders on the fire trucks

only reach the seventh floor."

What an interesting family.

* * * * *

It was lunch time at Memorial Park, and the parking lot around the tennis center was nearly full as it was the only public building where you could comfortably get out of business clothes and into running shorts before heading out to the track. Doug and I had been discussing the lawsuit on the phone for a couple of weeks, but neither of us could manage to get away for a run in the middle of the day. The weather was beautiful for Houston, since it was only 85 degrees, and Mondays were always slow days anyway. We had agreed to meet at 11:30, and it was five minutes till twelve. Just as I decided to take off running alone, Doug pulled in the driveway. It should not have been a surprise, but the sheer size of his brown Mercedes sedan made me wonder if it was custom-made.

We took off immediately, and it quickly became apparent that he was no slouch on the jogging trail. We ran at a little over a seven-minute-per-mile pace, and could still talk with little trouble. I wanted to find out about progress on the suit, but he kept bringing the conversation back to the tapes and Eternal Values.

A few days before our first run together, I had learned that his stepfather's company was in the throes of making one of the biggest commercial real estate decisions in Houston. They were nearing the expiration of their lease in Greenway Plaza and were actively in the market for almost 600,000 square feet of office space. The broker on that deal could expect to make at least $2.5 million dollars and maybe more if a complex series of transactions were required. More than ever before, I was intent upon making friends with the entire Wyatt family. If he wanted to talk about his religion, or for that matter anything, it was fine with me.

"I've got some books for you that Frederick wants you to read."

It was pretty impressive that a rich guy's guru would be sending me books.

"What are they?"

"It's a series by Ruth Montgomery. You need to read them in exactly the order I tell you."

"Fine."

As we went by the tennis center again, passing the three-mile mark, we came to a wooden deck where many of the thousands of runners per day stretch before taking off. Going by what I thought was a beautiful girl bending at a somewhat provocative angle, I commented on her athletic nature. Doug responded with what would later be an insight into his deepest beliefs.

"She's just perching her pussy."

"She's doing what?"

I really had not heard that particular explanation of female behavior before.

"Perching her pussy. . . .she needs to be pounded, and she's putting on a show to draw in a man to take care of her."

There was no ready response, so I just stayed quiet as we finished the last mile. While walking to cool down we talked about his dad's impending real estate deal, and he offered to bypass the entire bureaucracy at Coastal for a deal that I wanted to propose regarding the expansion of a building vacated by Prudential Insurance on the West Loop, not far from their existing location.

"You get the numbers ready, and I'll take it to dad when he gets back from Europe on Sunday. I'll go take him his coffee when he wakes up and get him to pay attention."

What I again assumed to be idle talk became reality two days later. He really did pitch the deal directly to his dad. Even though he wanted a big piece of the deal, there is no price too large to pay for direct access to the chairman of a major company, especially in a virtual autocracy like Coastal. What a great asset Doug was proving to be.

As we got back to the parking lot, Doug opened his car and pulled out five paperback books. He had numbered them on the cover page as to the sequence I was to read them. Once again the titles alone were compelling -- *Companions Along The Way, The World Before, A World Beyond, Strangers Among Us,* and *Aliens Among Us.*

Then, for the second time in the same hour, he surprised me by saying:

"This is deep metaphysical turf you're entering. If you ever say anything to anyone about it, I'll deny it. I'll just deny the whole thing. I'm good at that."

So why would a guy be ashamed or afraid of a religion he sincerely believed in? Rather than push it, I just told him what was essentially the truth:

"Look, Doug, I never talk to anyone about anything."

"I mean it, Roger, this is serious."

"So do I."

I mean, what could be more serious than a $2.5 million commission?

* * * * *

During the summer and fall of 1989 I spent a lot of time on Highway 401 between Toronto and Montreal researching land sites for Coca-Cola Foods. They were going to build their first Canadian packaging plant for Minute Maid, Five Alive, and their other juice drinks. It was a big deal to the people in eastern Ontario, and the countryside was beautiful, especially from a helicopter. It was a commercial real estate deal that was almost fun to do. The problem was that there were no direct flights into Toronto on Continental Airlines. I had fallen victim to the terminal illness of many business travelers, the frequent flyer program. Rather than miss the bonus miles of a long flight, I would fly to Detroit on Continental, sit for several hours, and then fly American or Air Canada into Toronto. As the father of two small children, husband of a medical intern, and sole revenue source for a business, the one thing that was missing in my life was quiet time to read. Shortly after Doug gave me the Montgomery books, I had to make two trips to Toronto. From the moment I sat down in the waiting area for the flight till we touched the ground in Toronto, I was buried in the strangest reading materials of my life.

From the beginning, Ruth Montgomery blew me away. She had serious literary credentials, having been a respected reporter and columnist for major newspapers and magazines. More importantly, she convincingly portrayed her personal contact with brilliant and devout people who have left their bodies on this planet, but have remained close in order to provide those of us that are still here with information that will help us attain our spiritual goals through understanding "The Beyond." Sure it was strange, but by the same token, I fully believed that Moses parted a great body of water with his hands and that God knocked Saul of Tarsus down in the road on the way to Damascus in order to give him a personal message. For that matter, I had clients and good friends leading respected lives who literally believed that Jonah had gotten into the belly of a whale and come out alive. Religion is not a logical thing.

By the time I got to the fifth book in the series that

Frederick von Mierers had prescribed and Doug Wyatt had delivered, Ruth Montgomery had herself become a prophet in my mind. Her stories were too bizarre to be fabricated, and she was too sincere to be discounted. It was the fifth book that was the key to formal entry into the recruiting maze of Eternal Values. In *Aliens Among Us*, Montgomery reveals that Frederick von Mierers and his top disciple, John Andreadis, were walk-ins, that is, great souls from history that have come back from other points in the universe to help prepare for great changes on the Earth in the coming years. She spent page upon page describing the high status of Frederick von Mierers with God and his critical importance to the establishment of leadership in the new age. According to her, Doug Wyatt's personal guru had been the high priest of Egypt in its Golden Age, the prophet Jeremiah in biblical times, and was now here to train a handful of leaders to help rebuild the planet after its virtual destruction at the millennium.

True or not, this was the most intriguing story I had ever encountered.

* * * * *

Shortly after I returned from Toronto, Doug and I met at Memorial Park, again on a Monday, for a combination of religion, business, and running. He looked strange, but he always looked a little strange. He didn't have much to say, other than a brief update on my lawsuit, and that he was really tired from his weekend trip to Eternal Values headquarters in New York.

"So how often do you go see Frederick and those people?"

"I'm up there every weekend, or close to them at my farm in North Carolina."

I started to ask if it wasn't a little expensive traveling that much but quickly remembered who I was talking to.

"What do you do?"

"We just enjoy each other, and cook. Frederick spends a lot of time reading to us from the Bible and the Hindu teachings. You really need to meet Frederick."

It was one of those lunchtime runs when you could see the sun devils dancing off the asphalt road, the temperature probably in the nineties. Running in the heat is no problem as long as you drink plenty of water before, slow down a bit from your normal pace, and just pay attention to what your body tries to tell you. Suddenly, just before we had completed four miles, Doug stopped abruptly and headed into the clump of trees just off the path.

"Are you okay, Doug? If you think you're having heat stroke, just lie down here in the shade, calm down, and I'll get some help."

"Don't say it. Don't even say heat stroke. It's just the fucking mushrooms."

Here I was, head of an organization that lobbied

companies to implement random drug testing in the workplace, and a guy who was rapidly becoming my really close friend was telling me that he was overheating due to a tough weekend of tripping on psychedelics with the prophet Jeremiah.

Heat stroke is serious business, and this was no time for a sermon on the evils of drugs. Doug just kept walking, and slowly the color came back into his face. After a half mile of walking in the shade, he appeared to be fine.

Always looking for intellectual or other equality with Doug, I figured it was time to let him gently know my current stand on illegal drugs. Drawing on my nearly forgotten days at Baylor College of Medicine:

"One of the problems with psychedelics is that they interfere with the thermoregulation mechanism in the preoptic region of the hypothalamus."

"What psychedelics?"

"You just told me five minutes ago that it was the mushrooms that were making you sick."

"No. No. No. . . .it was the mushrooms on my salad on the way back from New York last night."

It would be several months before Doug finally admitted that tripping was one of the essential components of the religious experience at Eternal Values, but he had already become adept at lying to me.

* * * * *

It was the day before vacation, and we were getting ready to head to Florida to burn up some of my Honored Guest awards from Marriott. In the weeks after the mushroom conversation at Memorial Park, Doug and I had made a transition to really being close friends. He had become a regular fixture at our house, and the kids loved him, especially my son. He would sometimes bring movies over for everyone to watch, many of which he said had been recommended by Frederick. They were always positive movies with a message, like "It's a Wonderful Life," or "The Never Ending Story." He never had much to say to my wife, but we had pretty much resigned ourselves to the fact that he was just an extremely lonely rich guy looking for a family. Shelly and I used to talk about which of her beautiful but starving medical school girlfriends would like to meet a tall, good-looking lawyer who was probably going to inherit fifty million dollars. The list was pretty long.

Doug had called the office to invite me to lunch. He said he needed to talk to me very badly. We had made some progress on getting Coastal's bureaucrats interested in my deal, and he had even used his father to get one of my clients some special attention in the $400 million sale of Houston Center, a multi-building and future development project in downtown Houston. When my client was ignored, Doug just had his dad pick up the phone at their ranch and call Dennis Hendricks, Chairman of Panhandle Eastern. It was fascinating to see how much more respect we got from the underlings.

In any event, he had reached a point of importance to me in a business sense that if he wanted to rearrange my schedule for a critical issue, it could certainly be accomplished. Doug always wanted to go to the same place for lunch, a health food restaurant called A Movable Feast on Alabama in the arty Montrose district. He was constantly giving me lectures on food combining, purified water, organic foods, and herbal supplements. He had even gotten me to start doing some shopping at a natural foods grocery store, which was conveniently located close to a McDonalds.

As usual, he was late. When he arrived, he was as excited as I had ever seen him.

"I have to have your address in Florida."

"Why? Is your dad going to send me a contract on the Prudential building?"

"Frederick has your life reading finished. He's going to send it to you tomorrow."

We had discussed the life reading on several occasions. According to Doug and his friends, it was a full history of your soul's progression, a sort of report card. Frederick von Mierers, who, Doug believed, had total access to all information, would go back to the earliest incarnations of an individual on the Earth, and follow the progress forward to today through all the lives and personalities that the soul in question had been or gone through. On the one hand, I figured that this was where the intriguing Hindu philosophy stopped, and the bullshit started.

On the other hand, Doug had continued to give me reading materials, including the works of Swami Vivekenanda, who had once headed Harvard Divinity School. The reading materials continued to be fascinating, and to their credit, Eternal Values had not asked me for a single penny.

Doug started to explain the significance of the life reading to me again, but one of his rich friends walked up, and he immediately switched gears. The friend was the son of famous Houston attorney Joe Jamail, who had recently kicked Texaco's butt to the tune of $3 billion on behalf of Pennzoil. According to the papers, Joe had made $600 million for himself in the process. The rest of the conversation centered around how difficult it was to find a good summer home in southern France for less than $50,000 per month. It was not a topic where I had a great deal of expertise, so I just finished my natural food cornbread and beans. It was still fascinating to me that Doug was terrified that any of his social circle might learn of the religion that was clearly the focal point of his life.

* * * * *

Nothing is more fun than playing par three golf with a four year old and a six year old. You play boys against girls with mom and dad doing the chipping and the kids doing the putting. Since the girls are better golfers, they win in the early going. But since dad had been on the wagon for over five years and mom was making a rare excursion into the land of Bud Light, the boys come out on top at the end of the game. It had been a great day, and thanks to the frequent stayer program of Marriott, we had a two-bedroom villa on one of the most beautiful beaches in Florida for free. The par three course was out our front door, and the beach was out our back.

When we went inside to get cleaned up for dinner, the message light was flashing on the phone. Federal Express had delivered a package to me. When the bellman drove up in his golf cart, I couldn't wait to hear the next step in my path into the psyche of this strange man from New York. Inside the overnight pouch were three tapes, simply titled Roger Hall I, Roger Hall II, and Introduction to the Beyond. After mom and the kids were asleep, I got out a Sony Sportsman and inserted Roger Hall I. For the next five hours, I spent time in the twilight zone.

Rather than the anticipated "You were Alexander the Great, and Julius Caesar, and . . .", accompanied by superficial glorification written by a palm reader, Frederick von Mierers spoke to me personally about a spiritual journey dating back to ancient China. The characters he developed as my various personalities were all people that I would like to have known, or been for that matter. Even equipped with the knowledge of my personality and behavior courtesy of Doug Wyatt, there was absolutely no way in the world that Frederick, or anyone else, could have known the mix of emotions and confusion in my mind regarding the search for God in a world of delusion. The tapes were a mix of the highest aspirations and the most degrading descriptions of behavior. Frederick was especially creative with regard to my ten-thousand-year history with women. In the same breath as a recounting of fascinating intellectual conversations with Voltaire would come revelations that at Versailles in the Court of Louis XIV, I had been famous for "pushing the bunny rabbits through the mattress, then getting up and leaving them moaning for the bone." By the end of the three tapes, I was completely drained emotionally. In the same manner as with the public tapes, but with an order of magnitude more complexity, Frederick von Mierers was trying as hard as he could to pull me into his psychotic web.

* * * * *

Doug and I made our pilgrimage to Memorial Park the day after I got back from vacation, and it was apparent that something had changed. He had no interest at all in the lawsuit and real estate deals that were usually the starting point of our conversations on the track.

"Do you realize how few people have had the opportunity to get this close to Frederick?"

I had no clue.

"I tell you what, Doug, whether it is all true or not, he is the most amazing character I've ever listened to. . . ."

"Roger, it's true. It's all true. You don't have an option now. If you come this close to the true path and don't follow through, you will destroy yourself."

"So, how does he know all this stuff?"

"Frederick reaches into the ether and pulls out anything he wants to know. The thing you have to understand is that you have to get the gems he prescribed right away. You are now a target for the Dark Forces, and none of us have a chance without them."

"How much are they?"

"The ones that I wear were about $150,000, but you don't need to get them all at once."

I had never paid a lot of attention to Doug's jewelry, but it struck me that it was quite a bit of money for evil spirit protection. For the first time, I began to wonder if the whole thing was a set up for a gem scam.

"So where does Frederick get these things?"

"Some of them we buy in the Antwerp and New York markets. Frederick gets incredible deals because he buys so many. The really important ones, like my opal, he just pulls out of the ether."

"That's a hell of a trick, Doug. Can he teach us how to do it?"

"Roger, this is not a joke. You have to get those gems as soon as you can. We don't have much time. Things are heating up, and people are getting to be more evil every day. You can't trust anyone but the Arcturians. Don't even think about it, just take a leap of faith. If you get this close and don't follow through, you'll end up just like my uncle."

"So how many Arcturians are there in Houston?"

"You and me, Roger."

Something else had changed. It was the first time that Doug had openly discussed his family with me. He told me that his brother Steve had reincarnated from Atlantis. Steve had been there in the final days before the destruction of Atlantis, and he would be destroyed again this time. He always found his way into favor with royalty but had no interest in anything but their money. Frederick had told him that his brother was an evil lost cause. His mother had bought her gems prescribed by Frederick and was trying desperately to overcome the fact that she was female, Jewish, and a Cancer astrologically. His stepfather, Oscar, was also a Cancer. Frederick had told him that because of their Astrological Sun Signs, they were both emotional wrecks, and their tumultuous relationship was due to this basic mismatch.

This was a lot to be dumped on me in three miles, so I changed the conversation back to business. JMB from Chicago was getting favored treatment on the Houston Center deal from Goldman Sachs Realty to the detriment of my client. Dark forces or not, Cancer or Prancer, I needed some more help from his dad.

* * * * *

That night, Doug stopped by to give me some files on the accounting records retrieved from his uncle, Robert Sakowitz. He had already spent two years and thousands of dollars on legal fees in an attempt to prove that Robert had plundered the Sakowitz business for himself. One of my hobbies was messing with computer graphics, so we were using two software systems for the Macintosh, Cricket Graph and Powerpoint, to help him chart out the flow of money through the various companies his uncle controlled prior to the bankruptcy and liquidation of the company.

Doug had gotten me to memorize two chapters from the Old Testament, the 23rd and 91st Psalms. He frequently told me, and in fact Frederick had said in my life reading, that the 91st Psalm is one of the most powerful writings in Western religion. We had started closing our eyes to say the two chapters out loud before we did any work, and also included the Lord's Prayer. It made sense to me to ask for divine help in business, especially in the "live and let die" world where I worked.

For some reason the air was charged with energy after we recited them together that night, and Doug began telling me the most incredible story I had ever heard. During his last trip to see Frederick he had learned that in their last incarnations his family had been together under different circumstances. His grandmother, Ann Sakowitz, had been a saloon owner in the old West. His stepfather, Oscar Wyatt, had been the sheriff in the town, and his uncle, Robert, had been a renowned villain and murderer that rampaged the territory. The stories he told me about Robert made Blue Duck in Larry McMurtry's *Lonesome Dove* sound like a cub scout master. Both his stepfather and uncle had fallen in love with his mother, Lynn Wyatt, who was one of the girls working for Ann. In a battle over her, Robert had killed his father. In this incarnation, it was Oscar's turn to get revenge, and it was Doug's divine task to help him.

This was finally too strange for me, but I needed Doug's access to his dad, and it was obvious that he was a really nice guy underneath all the strangeness. There was still no way for me to understand the power of the drugs Frederick von Mierers was using on Doug at every opportunity to plant and cultivate beliefs about his family that would build a wall between him and them.

I didn't say anything. Fortunately, my wife walked into the kitchen, and that was always a good way to get him to stop talking.

Before he left he made a strange request. It was the end of the month and billing time for his law firm. He told me that the mortgage payment was due on his farm, and he was out of cash. Would I write a check directly to him for the last month's hours spent on my lawsuit?

He left the study with $4,500 to pay his bill.

* * * * *

Doug and I saw each other almost every day during the last three months of 1989. His law firm had taken over all of my legal business, and I was even referring clients to them. He had become absolutely adamant about my going to see Frederick von Mierers in New York and never let any conversation pass without reiterating that my only hope of making it through the next ten years would be to buy the gems. In my life reading, Frederick had ordered me to wear a three-carat emerald, three-carat diamond, three-carat sapphire, five-carat cat's eye, four-carat opal, tourmolene, peridot, Chinese coral, lapus lazuli, and a bracelet made of gold, silver, copper, bronze, and platinum. It sounded like the year end inventory at Tiffany's. For months, I had successfully avoided the purchase by raising the issue of lack of money. However, as my attorney, Doug had learned of one of my deals that was throwing off large amounts of cash. Due to a referral of one of my clients to a European firm, I was getting thousands of dollars in wire transfers every month for virtually no effort. Doug knew that the coffers were filling at a fast rate.

By October of 1989, it was also becoming obvious that Goldman Sachs had their own agenda with regard to the sale of Houston Center, so I decided to go to New York to see if there was any hope of legitimacy in the sale. Doug had become involved as a principal in the deal, and he and I were to share ownership of a block of downtown Houston if we could pull it off, not to mention getting $1,850,000 in commissions and fees up front from our client. He was in New York the weekend before my trip and called me at home from Eternal Values headquarters on 54th street.

"Roger! Frederick wants to speak to you. He never talks to anyone anymore, but he will talk to you."

Over the course of the preceding months Doug had convinced me that this was akin to having your secretary tell you that the Pope is on line one, and Dan Rather is on line two to interview you after you talk to the Pope.

"Great, Doug."

He fumbled with the phone, and then Frederick said his first words to me:

"It is good to hear from you, my Lord. We have been together many times. You are an old friend and a great soul."

The prophet Jeremiah liked me.

"Thank you, Frederick. Doug has told me a lot of great things about you . . . ."

"I tell you, Roger, when I came into this body in 1978 it was such a horrible, atrocious mess. I would have to deal with this brain, and its constant urge to sit in front of the porno movies and beat off. It couldn't even get an erection because I was here."

This was not exactly the message one would expect from Jesus or Buddha, but it was a new age.

"You are coming to New York, Roger. You will come and stay with us, here in the apartments. We have a whole building. You are to be our guest."

"Thank you, Frederick, but I already have a reservation at the Essex House, and my clients are staying there as well."

"Then you will come to meet me."

"I look forward to it."

* * * * *

My meeting with Goldman Sachs did not start until four o'clock. After running seven miles around Central Park, I made all the phone calls that could be made given that most of the time zones were still asleep. Having read the *New York Times* and *USA Today* and had the traditional room service breakfast of pancakes, bacon, and a bagel for $17.50, there was not a hell of a lot left to do. The Essex House is right across the street from Central Park and is in the middle of an interesting group of hotels and bars, including the Ritz Carlton and my favorite place in New York, Mickey Mantle's sports bar. Even when on the wagon, it was fun to drink Perrier and look at the one of a kind photograph collection of Mickey, who had grown up only a few miles from my hometown. If there was any free time in the evening, my hobby was to put on blue jeans, sandals, and a tee shirt, then cruise Central Park South looking at all the extremely important and influential people rushing to extremely important and influential affairs in their extremely important and influential tuxedos and gowns. There is such simple joy in having people who make about half as much money as you do look at you like you are supposed to be on the other side of the street in the park scooping horseshit off the streets rather than walking on their sidewalk.

Surely the Eternal Values people were up as it was almost nine o'clock. Besides, if he was a real walk-in from space, Frederick von Mierers probably didn't sleep anyway. I pulled up the electronic Rolodex file for Doug Wyatt on my Macintosh portable computer and called the direct line to Frederick that Doug had given me. A very sleepy sounding Frederick answered the phone.

"Yes."

"Frederick, this is Roger Hall. Do you still want to meet today?"

"How are you, my Lord? I can see you at two o'clock."

After a split second thought of "Why would I wait five hours to see you?"

"Great, I'll see you then."

"Just tell the doorman you want apartment 4N, as in naturally high vibration."

"You're insane, Frederick. I'll see you at two."

I had unwittingly uttered the most prophetic words of my life.

* * * * *

Walking in New York has always been one of the great

intellectual challenges to me. The numbering of the streets is undoubtedly perfectly logical and easy for the natives, but after about forty-five minutes on what the concierge had told me would be a fifteen-minute walk, I once again submitted to utter failure and hailed a cab. He turned around in exactly the opposite direction, and had me at the door right on time. The complex at 405 East 54th appeared to be huge. It had a separate entrance and address on East 55th street and appeared to be in a good neighborhood.

My first clue as to the unique nature of my adventure came when I told the doorman that I was there to see Mr. von Mierers in 4N. From the look on his face, it was like telling him that it was a delivery of meat tenderizer for Jeffrey Dahmer. He just pointed to a nearby elevator without saying a word and quickly walked away.

The elevator was one of the old hydraulic variety with a once stylish dark wood interior and not quite sufficient fluorescent lighting. Apartment 4N was down in a corner, and there was nothing in the bland hallway that would have suggested the new world on the other side of the door. A young man, probably in his late teens, opened several locks, invited me in, and asked me to leave my shoes at the door. He was a strange little guy, bouncing rather than moving, and seemed to cower when he spoke to me.

"Frederick will be with you soon."

He disappeared through a door and left me to try to take

in the view. The ceiling was sky blue with wisps of white clouds streaking here and there. Michelangelo would have been proud of the paint job. The walls were all mirrors, polished to a point of perfection. The couch where I was placed was comprised of several pastel colors, none of which could have possibly matched, but looked really impressive together. Flowers were everywhere, and the room was filled with sounds - hypnotic Eastern music coupled with the constant background hum of machines that were purifying and humidifying the air. My attention soon came to rest on an absolutely stunning array of religious artifacts and symbols from virtually every faith. A gold Buddha smiled at me from across the room. On my right was a Star of David affixed to a mirror. Mother Mary held the Baby Jesus in a painting. Lord Krishna and the Divine Mother watched my every breath. It was an eclectic cathedral condensed to a twenty by twenty room.

    The little guy, who I had already nicknamed Tinkerbelle in my head, brought me a glass of what appeared to be dilute grapefruit juice in a lavender goblet. I had not asked for it, and he didn't ask if I wanted it. But as an obvious stranger in a very strange land, this was no time to offend the host.

    As soon as he left the room, Frederick entered from a hallway behind me. I am not a visual human, and in fact do not visualize at all, do not have any visual memory, or even care much what things look like. My world is a world of words and concepts. However, Frederick von Mierers immediately shattered my aversion to sight. He was tall, slender and if there had ever been a poster child for Aryan supremacy, it would have been Frederick. He was dressed entirely in white, except for his brown sandals. His face, however, belied a muscular atrophy that Doug had alluded to a couple of times. Doug claimed that Frederick suffered from a persistent, and virtually untreatable skull infection as the result of an automobile accident. From my first look at him, I thought Frederick was dying of AIDS.

He seated himself without shaking hands on a small ottoman across the room from me. Buddha looked at me from over the top of his head.

"You look exactly as I knew you would, my Lord. You got fat in Rome after you made your money, and you are getting fat again. If you would just let go of that stubborn ego and follow the diet that Douglas has given you, you would be a warrior again."

So much for introductions.

"Thank you for taking the time to see me. . ."

It was the last thing that I would say for an hour and a half. Frederick immediately began a dissertation which he told me in the beginning was a personal one from God about my role in the fate of the world over the next ten years.

My life has been filled with brilliant people. My wife of twenty years breezed through M.D. and Ph.D. programs with no effort. I was able to spend a little time at Baylor College of Medicine in Houston with people who are or will be Nobel Prize candidates. In business, it had been my good fortune to work directly with men like Doug Ivester, the cordial genius who is heir apparent to the throne of Roberto Goizueta at Coca-Cola, and Larry Hilblom, the H in DHL, who had taken his only $500 in 1968 and turned it into a personal net worth in excess of $2 billion by the end of 1991.

Frederick von Mierers, by a great distance, was the most intellectually overpowering human being that I had ever met.

He lectured me on the international political situation, the world economy, Hindu scripture, the book of Revelation, God's rationale for destroying the Earth as it now exists, New York real estate, gourmet cooking, and the Egyptian mystical tool of "thought transference." He claimed that at Geza in the temple of the high priest, Ptahotep, I had been a brilliant student of the technique and literally able to create my environment simply with thought.

On several occasions, I tried to say something. When the first few words were out of my mouth, Frederick would immediately answer the question that was about to be asked and then proceed to answer every related question in the train of thought. It occurred to me that when I was young there had been a book about John von Neumann, the brilliant scientist, that had described his ability to do exactly the same thing. It was simultaneously fascinating and frightening. No matter what Frederick was, he was a damned sight smarter than me.

About halfway through the ninety-minute lecture,

Tinkerbelle brought in two huge African parrots. They had been making loud cat-like sounds in an adjacent room and looked as if they could serve as palace guards. The minute the first one was placed on his shoulder, Frederick turned his head and let the parrot stick its long, skinny tongue inside his mouth. He rotated on the little sofa and did the same thing with the other parrot. The smartest guy I had ever met, the Messiah according to my attorney and best friend, was French kissing a fucking parrot. Once again, there was nothing to do but sit. It had taken thirty-five years to produce the moment when I had nothing to say at all.

After the short excursion into beak smooching, he immediately began another discourse, this time on the gems and my role in the life of Doug Wyatt.

"Douglas says you won't buy the gems. When you return, he will show you his mother's appraisal. She made $150,000 beyond the $75,000 she paid. It will be the best financial investment you have ever made, my Lord. I can get them for nothing. I make nothing. I need nothing. People come here to offer me gifts or to build a beautiful mansion for me to live in. All they really want is to control me. I cannot be controlled. I tell them that they can build the mansion if they promise to never come there. Then they go away."

He had touched on the topic of Douglas' mother, international socialite Lynn Wyatt, and for the first time he truly embarrassed me by proudly recounting a section of her life reading.

"I said, Mrs. Wyatt, you don't want to get fucked by an Italian truck driver, you want to get fucked by the truck."

It was beyond me that anyone would say that to a friend's mother, especially one whose husband is liable to kick your butt or sue you until you can wallpaper your house with subpoenas. But both Doug and his former escort, Susan Bearden, confirmed the story. Susan would later tell me that Doug would often sit for hours studying Lynn Wyatt's life reading in order to better understand how to manipulate her for money. When I asked Doug about the comment, he said it was just Frederick's way of getting people to focus on their true sexual nature.

"You have a great choice to make, Roger. You will be wealthy and successful no matter what you do, but successful to what end? Douglas will lead the world into a thousand years of unparalleled peace and prosperity. Help him, and you will take your rightful place in history. Fail, and you will live through the hell that will come, your children will die, and you will be forced to teach the orphans of the destruction why it happened."

I had no clue what to say or do. This strange character had totally overpowered me intellectually, told me the most interesting story of my life, and then threatened me with the worst nightmare of any parent. Should I kill him, believe him, or simply go away?

For the first time, I spoke.

"Frederick, it's three forty-five, and I have to be down on

Wall Street by four."

In a tone of subdued disgust, "Yes, go to your meeting."

He followed me to the door, took both of my hands in his hands, and in a deadly serious tone repeated: "God bless you, God bless you, God bless you, God bless you, God bless you."

"God bless you, Frederick."

* * * * *

I don't remember much of the meeting at Goldman Sachs, other than it was a big floor full of young, aggressive MBAs led by a young, aggressive female MBA. They had clearly decided who was in the deal before it started, and my client and I were not. It didn't make a whole hell of a lot of difference. I was sure glad to see LaGuardia airport.

* * * * *

One of my many character flaws is to deal with difficult emotional problems by pretending they don't exist. I quickly wrote off the troublesome comments of Frederick and remembered only that he was an obvious genius and, alien or not, one of the most impressive scholars on religion anywhere.

Doug had reached a point of absolute compulsion regarding my getting the gems. Three things began to work to my detriment -- Doug, my first regular friend in a long time, was sincere about his beliefs; there was plenty of cash lying around my wholly owned Subchapter S corporation; and, most importantly, his mother, one of the richest women in the world and I assumed one of the most astute with regard to gems, had purchased the same things and made a bunch of money.

In December, I agreed to give Doug $44,000, part immediately, and the rest following receipt of a deal that finally closed in May of 1990. He was absolutely ecstatic.

The curious thing was that he insisted on blank money orders, and I would get no receipt. He also hit me up for another $4,000 check made directly to him rather than his firm for legal work.

I was personally terrified of the IRS and always paid the maximum tax on my income. Writing a $200,000 check for the federal government to distribute to fifth-generation welfare recipients hurt, but it was better than fighting something that could not be beaten. Doug openly told me that he and the other members of the organization never paid any tax, even though Eternal Values generated millions of dollars in profit from sales of materials and gems. That was his business.

We met at A Movable Feast for lunch, and I gave him the first batch of money orders. He was off to New York for the weekend and carried the money away to the Messiah in his tailored vest pocket.

* * * * *

Doug's mistake, and perhaps the biggest mistake of his life, was in thinking that by getting money, I had made the transition to total compliance with his beliefs. Getting money must have been a special step for Frederick's sales force, because Doug got weird quick. On many occasions, we had invited him to come over and watch movies with the family in the evening. In many ways, he was just a big kid. His favorite movie was still "The Never Ending Story," and it became a favorite of my kids after he brought it over for us to watch. One night, after seeing the movie again, and shortly after he had gotten my money, we were sitting in the family room talking after my wife and kids had gone to bed. He said, out of context and without warning:

"The angels watch and giggle when I beat off."

Not having a ready reply, I moved the conversation back to the more mundane topic of world affairs. We came to a point in our discussion about his lawsuit against Uncle Robert later in the evening that required the use of one of the computers in my study, so I went to my seat behind a massive oak desk and turned on the Macintosh II and my color plotter. With no warning whatsoever, Doug had gotten up from his chair, walked around the desk, and gotten down on his knees on the floor beside me. When I turned around to ask him which file to pull up, he put one hand on either arm of my desk chair and looked up at me with a look that I had, quite frankly, never seen before. It was a good way for an aggressive heterosexual to learn compassion for girls who claim to have been victims of date rape. I was simultaneously shocked, scared, furious, and speechless. There is no way for me to know how I looked, but evidently it was not inviting because he immediately fell back, put his hands together in a prayerful position, and told me how wonderful it was to be my friend. He got up, walked back to his chair, and it never happened again. It was this event that led to my response in the *Wyatt v. Sakowitz* deposition that "You don't have the right to hate all homosexuals anymore than you have the right to hate all Jews," to which attorney David Berg replied "Amen." But you should have the right to pound them in the face if they make the same mistake twice. Doug never did.

* * * * *

It was tough to learn that Doug was gay, or at least bisexual, but his dad still had a bunch of real estate, and he was still a nice guy. The incident in the study never repeated itself, partially because I refused to meet with him alone anymore, and over the course of the early months of 1990, we had become involved in even more business deals together. He showed me a different kind of strangeness in the restructuring of a commission agreement on an office lease deal that was to net me several hundred thousand dollars over ten years. The owners of the building were extremely tough, would probably screw you if they could, and were therefore no different than almost every other landlord I met. Doug's problem with them was that they were Jewish. I had gone to Hartford to meet them and actually liked the principals, a couple of self-made millionaires who started with nothing and worked their butts off.

They messed with me a little bit on an expansion of the tenant's lease, and I asked Doug how to handle it.

"The only way to deal with Jews is to totally humiliate them. Subconsciously, that is what they want, and unless you just pound them into total submission, they will just come back and do it all to you again."

"That's bullshit, Doug."

"Look, I've been meaning to give you some more books Frederick thinks you need. I'll drop them by tonight."

He proceeded to raise all kinds of hell with the developer, taking some confidential information I had about their misuse of partnership funds and beat them over the head with it. It was vicious, but they sure paid up in a hurry.

He came by that night, but didn't stay long. After the incident in the study, our friendship had become a little strained. I had professional friends who were gay, and although I am not homophobic, it was a great disappointment to me to learn that Doug didn't have the guts to just tell me. Hell, we were supposed to be close friends.

The books he left were by Henry Ford, and he told me that they were the most complete and factual account of what he was trying to prove to me about modern-day Jews. Doug outlined a

Jewish plot to control the international media and banking industries, infiltrate the United States Treasury Department, and ultimately force all non-Jews into servitude.

For the very first time, I knew that something was seriously wrong with the only close friend I had in Houston.

The books laid in the same position on the desk in my study for two weeks, and he finally came to pick them up. My psychological state was going to hell in a hand basket. Doug was not only gay, he had somehow failed to take a good look at my nose during our affiliation. My great grandmother was a full-blooded Jewish immigrant and must have been the first in the family to have adopted the renegade attitude. She had married an Irish Catholic, moved to Arkansas, and I assume escaped the wrath of both sides of that religious mismatch. I was a disenfranchised Jew, certainly not ashamed of it, nor convinced that my ancestors were the incarnation of evil. Additionally, my best friend out of Houston was a surgeon who was fully Jewish. We had drank enormous quantities of beer and harassed each other for years. He frequently told me that if my great-grandmother hadn't screwed up, I might have been able to get a good job instead of just a few packages at Christmas. Finally, and probably most importantly, the finest man in the commercial real estate business in Houston, Texas is, Martin Fein. In all my years in the real estate community, he had treated me better than anyone else. Once when my young company was having a cash flow crisis, Martin had paid me four months early on a commission and saved me a bunch of trouble. He was the head of the Anti-Defamation League, and his parents had been victims of the Holocaust. Doug was trying to convince me that Martin was part of a demonically evil conspiracy. What really bothered me was that Doug hung out in the same social circle as Martin and was cordial to his face. I had even brought Doug and Martin together on one of the ploys to buy Houston Center. Part of being a renegade was disgust for hypocrisy.

*****

Turmoil had become a constant state of affairs inside my head during the early months of 1990. Even though Doug was showing signs of being a couple of bricks shy of a full load, and Frederick was even more strange, I had become progressively more influenced by Frederick's taped dissertations on the universe and had actually made an intellectual commitment to Hinduism as a result of the books from Eastern philosophy and religion.

It is painful for a loner to give up a friend, even if there is substantial evidence of a problem. He had delivered my ring and some other gems with certified appraisals that clearly showed a profit. The ring, a beautiful Egyptian design of 18K gold with a central seven-carat sapphire, two four-carat emeralds, and two three-carat topaz had cost me $35,000. The certified appraisal Doug delivered to me showed it was worth

$90,000. I would do that deal all day long.

Doug had even taken steps to try to introduce me into the social world of his family. We had met at a club near his office one day for a lunchtime six-mile run through Houston's stately River Oaks area. It was one of those not so unusual hot January days in the city, and as we made a turn in front of River Oaks Country Club, he told me to come with him to the gate of his parents' mansion, which is next door to the country club.

"This is Douglas."

The iron gate swung open, and we ran up the driveway to the kitchen entrance of the Wyatt home. When one of the maids opened the door, it was like a scene from the Old South. There was a huge black woman sitting on a stool over an ancient stove, making a turkey for Doug to take with him to New York that afternoon. She obviously thought a lot of Doug, and they chatted back and forth for a minute about why she did or did not need to use reverse osmosis purified water to cook his food.

I was in a state of generalized shock. Looking out of the kitchen, it was obvious that Versailles, which was my only reasonable comparison, would make a good second home if this were your primary residence. The house was filled with beautiful art, crystal chandeliers, and antique furniture. There were no visible signs of human habitation. It was like stopping to get some water at the National Gallery of Art.

Doug actually let me go out the front door, and, as we left, he made a comment that I will never forget:

"You shouldn't think differently of me because of this."

"You told me it was just an illusion, Doug."

"It is."

We didn't say anything else on the return run.

* * * * *

All hell broke loose in March 1990.

The March 1990 edition of *Vanity Fair* signaled great trouble for Doug. The once-secretive Frederick von Mierers agreed to an interview with writer Marie Brenner. The only conceivable explanation for this last suicidal bout with arrogance was that he died of AIDS shortly before the article came out. Since complications of AIDS frequently include neurological devastation, it is possible that his physical condition was responsible for the tremendous strife he created for his followers. The article was full of revelations on the real nature of Eternal Values -- stories of bisexual orgies, organized theft, drug use, violence, and rabid enforcement of a neo-Nazi philosophy.

During the aftermath, my wife and I struggled to recover from the psychological shock of the revelations of ex-members about Doug. Even though it was dreadfully apparent that Doug was involved in something far more evil than we had ever expected, we helped him during the aftermath of the publication, which included the physical debilitation of his mother for several days.

The day "East Side Alien" hit the stands, Doug came straight to our house. He was terrified. His mother had gotten advance notice and had been in bed throwing up for three days. We tried everything to get him back together. I took him down to Braes Bayou for a run. We went to his favorite health food restaurant and got him some take-out food. My wife even told him that once his mother figured she was losing weight she would thank him. Nazi or not, we still cared for the guy.

Doug was soon strong enough to lie to everyone again, especially us. He told us that the article was the result of a Jewish bitch writing lies about their organization based on half-truths from disgruntled former members and employees. He and his mother quickly adopted a story line that blamed the entire thing on his girlfriend, Susan Bearden. Doug got his mother to tell her socialite friends that Susan had been a member, he had not, and he had been unfairly indicted by affiliation.

It blew over for Doug fairly quickly, and the old guys he saw at his father's club just wanted to know if he had been able to nail any of the models. His dad just assumed it was another hatchet job by the press.

*****

The pressure was building inside me. On March 22, 1990, I

had finished a day's work in Alabama for Hormel. I was headed back to Montgomery for an early flight the next morning to Atlanta for a meeting with the new director of real estate for Coca-Cola. I had been clean and sober for more than five years, run a marathon and found a new religion full of knowledge and hope, which I then discovered was a front for the very essence of evil.

I pulled off the road and entered the Blue and Gray lounge. I have no memory of coming out.

* * * * *

There was still business to be done with Doug, and I had set up a lunch with my new business partner to meet him. We were sitting at a table at Evan's, the new high-end health food restaurant in town, discussing an unusual deal that had arisen unexpectedly. I had been working with Coca-Cola Foods, the $2.5 billion division of Coca-Cola for years, and had a wide variety of friends within the company. They had a long history in Houston, and the acquisition of their national headquarters building in the Galleria area had been one of my projects on their behalf.

Coca-Cola Foods' management group was feeling a lot of heat from the parent company in Atlanta. The company was extremely profitable by the standards of almost any analyst but not by the standards of Coca-Cola. There had been rumors of sale of the division for quite a while, but now the CFO had approached me about setting up two meetings for him -- one with Drew Craig, a friend of mine and former member of Boone Pickens' inner circle at Mesa Petroleum, and another with Doug to establish a line of communication with his stepfather. They were actively soliciting financial backing for a management led leveraged buy-out of their company.

Having read about Oscar Wyatt's handling of Mike Milken on the acquisition of American Natural Resources, I was reluctant to count on any big fees from Coastal or the Wyatts in the event they organized the financing. But the real deal for me was that the CFO made it clear that if the deal came together, they would immediately sell almost 25,000 acres of orange groves in Florida in order to pay down the debt of the takeover. I would be the exclusive agent for disposition, and the gross value of the sale would be roughly $400 million. Once again, Doug might be the key to my retirement plan.

Doug called me at the office that afternoon.

"I talked to dad, and he says it's a good company. He can do the deal with three phone calls, but you need to get those managers to realize that not only are managers a dime a dozen but that there is no such thing as a hostile management led buy-out. They need to be up front with Atlanta, or it won't work."

"How much do we make?"

"What does he need us for? It has to be on the groves. You need to get a contract now that gives you agency even in the event of a change of ownership."

"That's tough, but I'll try."

"Roger, if you would just take a leap of faith and buy the rest of your gems, all these things would just come to you."

"It's been tight here, Doug. I'm trying to get organized to take over downtown."

"You look puffy, Roger. Are you drinking again?"

"Just a bit. But not excessive. By the way, I have the rest of your money from the first batch of gems."

"I'll come by tonight."

* * * * *

We had very little to say to each other. It was mid-May 1990, and the storm over *Vanity Fair* had blown over for Doug. He was showing serious signs of frustration with my lack of cooperation on the diet he had given me and especially with the fact that I wouldn't buy the rest of the gems. I assumed he had given up on me as a sexual target as well. The only common interest we had left was money.

"I get bored with people easily, Roger."

"Yeah, I know. So what happens if I tell you that the Eternal Values thing is looking a little too strange. . . ."

"We'll drift apart."

For the first time, it became clear that what I had hoped to be a life long friendship was contingent upon a lot of things that

I had no intention of doing. From the moment I knew who Doug was, I had gone out of my way to avoid looking like he was a target for money. On a hundred occasions he had told me about people using him to get to his mom or dad. My slate was clean with regard to cash at that point. Counting the gems, direct legal fees, and loans for his farm payments when times were tight, I had given Doug more than $75,000 in cash. He had never given me a thing, except for some coffee cups and a juicer.

"So, what do we do about the deals, Doug."

"We get the money."

At least that part of his heart was still in the right place.

Doug took the money orders for the gems I owed him and walked out the door of my house for the last time. Maybe business just wasn't the right place to make friends.

That night I read the *Vanity Fair* article for the very first time. It was terrifying. If even half of it were true, Doug was a central figure in one of the most evil organizations imaginable. The article reported that lots of people had gotten certified appraisals on their gems like mine and Lynn Wyatt's. The problem was that they came from crooked appraisers that Frederick von Mierers had paid off. A trip to Louis Tennebaum, Houston's premier estate jeweler, the next day confirmed my worst fears. The gems Doug had sold me for $44,000 were worth a maximum of $10,000. My best friend had stolen a total of $65,000 from me. It was time for a serious conversation.

* * * * *

Doug had agreed to have breakfast with me at Le Peep, a quiet restaurant a few blocks from my house. It was 7:30, and we were to have met at seven.

"Sorry I'm late."

"You're always late."

"Dad wants to do that Coca-Cola Foods deal. . . ."

"Look, Doug, I don't want to talk about business. I want to talk about these gems you sold me."

He immediately turned icy.

"What about them?"

"Louis Tennebaum tells me that the ring is worth about $7,500 and the rest are essentially worthless."

"I've seen this happen time and time again."

"People getting fucked over by your friends. . . ."

"No. When you stop believing that the gems are worth what they are worth, they lose their value."

"Are you telling me that I lost $35,000 because I don't believe your rocks are magic?"

"What's wrong with you, Roger?"

"I'm completely fucking furious, Doug. I don't care if you're gay. I don't care if your rich and scared to death someone is going to make you buy lunch. I don't care if your daddy owns the fucking moon. But I thought we were friends, and you ripped me off for your faggot buddies in New York. Not to mention fucking with my mind over God. . . ."

"Are you drinking again?"

"You bet. But I'm not getting pounded in the ass by a bunch of neo-Nazi fairies from outer space, and my liver will last a hell of a lot longer than your reamed asshole buddies."

"Calm down. People are looking."

"What the fuck do you care? They're just an illusion anyway."

"Roger, those gems stopped being worth anything when you stopped believing they were worth anything."

In a story that would get a chuckle from his mother, Lynn Wyatt, when I called her several months later. I picked up the salt shaker from the table and said:

"Well, I tell you what. I believe that this salt shaker is worth a million bucks. You write me a check, and then I'll believe it's worth two million so we can both make some money."

Doug got up and headed for the door. I followed him outside and stopped him a few steps away from his car.

"Look, Doug. If you ever want to get away from those people, I'll personally pay for your deprogramming. Those people are taking you for a big ride."

"Fuck you."

For the first time since I had known him, Doug showed some signs of being capable of physical violence. I knew that he had a personal arsenal of handguns that Frederick had told him to get, and I moved to block his access to the car door.

"I want my money back, Doug. I'll sell those things to you for exactly what you charged me."

"For God's sake, Roger, look at yourself. The Dark Forces have gotten you. You will end up just like my uncle. Get back on the path while there is still time."

"It's bullshit, Doug. It's a gem scam, and you either pay me back and get some deprogramming or I'll blow the whistle on the whole deal."

"Remember what Frederick told you about your children, Roger."

"You touch my kids, and you and your faggot buddies will be praying for the end of the world."

He pushed me out of the way. I could have killed him with my hands, and I wanted to. He had stolen money from me in the names of God and friendship, then he made what was most certainly the worst mistake of his life by threatening my kids. Doug's life was going to take a turn downhill.

* * * * *

In many ways, John Andreadis is the most interesting and tragic of the characters I tracked down to learn the real story on Doug and Eternal Values. The brilliant son of a wealthy New York family, he, like most of Frederick von Mierers victims, was fascinated at an early age by religion in general and Hindu philosophy in particular. Unfortunately for John, he ran head on into Frederick in 1979 at a metaphysical bookshop in Manhattan. He was sixteen years old. Within weeks, Frederick had convinced John of his status as a holy man, turned him against his own family, and set him on a course that would ultimately steal ten years of his life, during which he would be exalted, manipulated, beaten, ripped apart emotionally and psychologically, and according to his former wife, probably infected with the AIDS virus.

By the time I was introduced to the Eternal Values program by Doug Wyatt, John had already made the ultimate error of objecting to the ever-increasing insanity of Frederick and his inner circle. As John has said in public interviews, "Frederick had gone berserk, and no one could control him anymore." For his disagreement, he was beaten in front of the inner circle, having his face smashed again and again on Frederick's always immaculately clean pink marble floors. A tape of the beating was distributed to the membership, explaining that after ten years of holding a status equivalent to that of the Apostle Peter in Christianity, he was denounced as the forerunner of the AntiChrist. For centuries, Andreadis had reincarnated again and again with Frederick, each time holding great potential for good, but each time falling ultimately to the dark forces. When I later asked Doug about the logic of a peace-loving holy man smashing the face of a former exalted follower, he said: "Frederick did it out of love. It was his last attempt to save John from his own ego."

For God knows what reason, John ended up in Houston working at a stock brokerage company in early 1990, just as I was becoming aware of the real reasons for Doug Wyatt's eighteen-month-long recruiting process on me. Before our confrontation Doug came over to my house one evening to discuss the lawsuit against his uncle, he had been literally as white as a ghost. He had walked into A Movable Feast to get some dinner and come face to face with Andreadis. With no idea that John was in Houston, Doug, in his mind, had unwittingly stepped before the right-hand man of the AntiChrist. He dropped his tray, ran to the car, and was still shaking by the time he got to my house. It took over an hour for him to regain his composure. Such was the nature of Frederick's ability to control a victim's opinion of an exile.

After my confrontation and disassociation with Doug, I called John, and he was terrified to even speak to me. Finally, after hours of telephone discussion, when he was finally comfortable that my intent was to simply find out about the inner circle and its behavior, he agreed to meet. We met three times in all, and it became clear that John had individually been the intellectual force that had propelled Frederick to the point where he could get someone like Pete Olson, former head of IBM's Latin American division, to give him $100,000 in blank money orders for $10,000 worth of jewels without batting an eye.

For ten years John was the genius in the back room,

working eighteen to twenty hours a day studying ancient Hindu writings, preparing the scripts for the life readings that Frederick recited and then sold to thousands of subscribers, including Sylvester Stallone and Rae Dawn Chong, for $350 apiece and constantly expanding the base of information that came together to produce an intellectual web that would trap thousands of individuals around the world. When he was eighteen, John was sent to Massachusetts to live in virtual isolation as he prepared the initial set of cassette tapes that became the informational backbone of Frederick's empire. As Frederick amassed millions of dollars in revenue from his sales of religious writings, tapes, life readings, and gems, John was given spending money and a place to sleep.

The only frightening moment in my conversations with John came when we looked out the window of the study in front of my house into the twilight of evening. A brown Mercedes, driven by Doug, slowed to a near stop in front of my yard, paused for a moment as its driver peered in the window, and then sped quickly away. When I looked back at John, he was shivering and crying like a man who had just looked his own death in the face.

John was my first insight into the total control the group exercised over Doug. Since Frederick's death shortly before the publication of the *Vanity Fair* article, Doug had ascended to share the top position in the cult. John still talked to friends in New York who had access to information about the inner circle.

He spilled his guts about the gem scam and the hidden agenda of the membership when dealing with outsiders like me. The one thing that he did not tell me I learned later. Most of John's terror of disclosure was the result of his own participation in the bizarre homosexual behavior of the cult. I would later learn from Susan Bearden that Frederick had once brought in a black bisexual marine, put a pile of *Bhagavad Gitas* on the floor, and made John lay on them while the marine had anal sex with him as a group of ten other male members sat on couches and masturbated while enjoying the show.

I continue to believe that John was recruited to be a homosexual. When he was meeting with me in Houston, he was dating a topless dancer and seemed to be quite happy having sex with girls. Once again, I had new ammunition for my war with Doug and his cult. John Andreadis had no way of defending himself at age sixteen from Frederick and his madmen. As far as I was concerned, the kids on the streets of New York and Lake Lure, North Carolina near cult operations centers were helpless targets too.

* * * * *

The worst day of Doug Wyatt's life occurred on Wednesday, May 15, 1990. He didn't have any clue that it was a bad day.

For months I had been trying desperately to make contact

with Susan Bearden. Doug had kept her modeling shots from the Ford Agency on the credenza of his office, and she always accompanied him to major social events like the Wyatt family hosting Duchess Sarah Ferguson at their ranch. After *Vanity Fair* came out, Doug told me that she had flipped out, like any woman would under pressure, and moved to Europe. I assumed that if anyone knew what Doug was really up to she would. After fifty calls to the Ford Agency, she finally returned my call. If ever terror has been transmitted over international telephone lines, that was the day. She was scared to death, and, knowing that Doug had been my friend, she assumed that he was using me to find out where she was, and what she was doing.

After weeks of assurance and conversation, she and her new husband had agreed to meet with me during their trip to the United States in May. On Wednesday, May 15, 1990, I boarded Continental Airlines flight 1150 for Atlanta at eight in the morning. Before returning that same afternoon at three, my life would change forever.

* * * * *

Susan Bearden is devastatingly beautiful. She epitomizes the concept of a southern belle. The gentle accent indicative of her Carolina upbringing, coupled with a real and apparent sensitivity to all those around her magnify the physical beauty. I never knew what the Ford Agency was until the March 1990 edition of *Vanity Fair*, but if they deal as I understand in the representation of models like Susan, it must be a great way to make a living.

When we met in Atlanta, she had recently married a German Air Force officer who knows all of her skeletons, loved her without reservation, and had a strong and in my opinion, perfectly justified interest in killing anyone associated with the Eternal Values organization. Doug Wyatt's life insurance carrier needs to prepare a rider that requires him to stay at least as far away from him as the travel range of Germany's state of the art fighter jet at any given time.

In the August 22, 1991, edition of the *Houston Press*, editor Tim Fleck flippantly refers to some of the details of my deposition as *Wyatt v. Sakowitz* in the "Twilight Zone." My four hours with these two people fighting to rebuild a life that should never have been destroyed could accurately be described as the twilight zone experience of my life. Most of what I learned appears nowhere in the deposition, and out of respect for and camaraderie with these two, I would have risked perjury to avoid sharing most of Susan's story with the attorneys, and therefore the world at large.

For two years, Susan accompanied Doug to give him the respected illusion of heterosexuality as he served as the eyes and ears for Frederick von Mierers into the affairs of his own family. Frederick wanted to know every detail of the lives of the family that he saw as his first class ticket to the international social and business circles that would become the ultimate breeding ground for his neo-Nazi empire.

It was the four hours with Susan and her husband that drove me over the edge. Had it not been for her tears and rage, I might have not taken the steps that led to the deposition that destroyed my business and reputation. For the first time, someone was telling me the absolute truth about what went on behind the closed doors at Eternal Values. Within ten minutes, it was clear that Doug was living a double life and that Eternal Values was a rich kid's homosexual dream club. In story after story, she left me totally dumbfounded by the knowledge that the guy who had been my friend was a raging gay queen in the confines of von Mierers' apartments. She would tell me in later conversations that Douglas had been ordered by Frederick to settle my lawsuit handled by his firm, even though Doug had made it clear to him we could win at trial based on a letter agreement in my records. He had betrayed me in the worst fight of my business life at the orders of his guru.

But it was one story that pushed me permanently over the edge, and created a war to the death between Doug and myself. Susan had been in the apartments when Doug had arrived with my first set of money orders for gems. Frederick praised Doug lavishly for his success, and Doug announced to the assemblage:

"Roger Hall wants it in the ass, and he just doesn't know it!" to the delighted shrieks of his fellow members.

I don't recall much of what Susan said after that, although the stories are recorded in many hours of audio tape generated about Doug and Eternal Values in subsequent months.

I was already totally consumed in planning the destruction of Doug Wyatt and his sick cult.

* * * * *

Legal malpractice just has to be the next great growth industry in this country. Sure there are some good lawyers that serve viable functions to the betterment of society. There are also serial killers that you would enjoy going out with for a game of pool and a beer. But not a lot.

It occurred to me that perhaps Doug had breached his legal and ethical responsibility as my attorney by getting me to settle a lawsuit that should have been won so that he could have the money, selling me investment gems that he knew were worthless, lying to me about his involvement in a sinister cult, demanding direct payments for legal services to the detriment of his partners, using illegal psychedelic drugs while acting as my counsel, and demanding participation in real estate transactions and other deals thereby effectively peddling influence through manipulation of his stepfather. This could not possibly be acceptable behavior, even for lawyers.

Of course, what I was really upset about was the fact that he thought he could turn me into a pervert like himself, but that was probably legal. I had to be more realistic in my allegations.

Having never used a litigator other than Doug, I was off in search of someone to sue him and his law firm for me. My very first thought was that the guy representing Doug's uncle, Robert Sakowitz, probably didn't like Doug, and might be willing to work for me.

I didn't expect much interest from Bobby Sakowitz when asking him for a referral but, when he heard the reason, he immediately began talking like my new best friend and wanted to have breakfast together the next day.

* * * * *

Bobby Sakowitz called the Buffalo Grille, home of Houston's best blueberry pancakes, to tell me that the nanny's bus had been late, and he was running behind. Already he was more responsible than his nephew. Besides, he was only fifteen minutes late when he did arrive.

Bobby was the only son of Bernard Sakowitz and, in good Jewish family tradition, inheritor of the family business. Unfortunately for him, he chose to expand the empire in the glory days of the late 1970s prior to the depression that engulfed Texas in the 1980s. Some say he ran the revered retail empire into the ground. My opinion is that Bobby was simply the victim of market forces beyond his control, as were so many others in the oil and real estate businesses in the Texas depression of the 1980s.

Although Doug was suing him for breach of fiduciary obligation to his trust fund (the primary asset had been now worthless Sakowitz stock) Bobby's principal crime was that he was a Jew. But he was a Jew who halted his own life to help raise Doug Wyatt and his brother Steve after the reported suicide of their natural father, who had been in jail for strangling a young woman to death while under the influence of LSD.

It was the harmless breakfast at the Buffalo Grille in Houston that triggered a bizarre series of events.

Bobby Sakowitz is not my kind of guy. He worries too much about his hair, suits, shoes, and fingernails for my tastes, but he was obviously not evil. My gut level perception was that one of the reasons he ran into trouble was that he wasn't mean enough, especially in dealing with predators like L.J. Hooker International that fed on the remnants of his father's empire when the blood was in the water. At one point, following my explanation of Doug's failed attempt to recruit me into his cult and my quest for revenge, he even said something that gave me an insight into why people like Bobby fight so hard to get where they are and to do the things that they do. When I asked him how he had managed to get so crosswise with his brother-in-law, he said: "Oscar dislikes anyone who was born with any advantage, since he wasn't. But Oscar didn't have to be the only Jew in a private high school in Houston, Texas. Every day, everywhere I went I heard 'Here comes the jewboy'."

He was anxious to have me meet his attorney, a guy named David Berg. Berg, one of Houston's most prestigious attorneys, called that very afternoon to arrange an appointment.

*****

If you ever get really, really pissed off and want to spend a bunch of money on the world's meanest mad dog lawyer to help you get even, be sure to put David Berg on your list of people to interview. David is one of those rare people who sincerely believe that everything standing between him and where he is going at any given time needs to either get out of his way, help him, or die.

In my life prior to meeting David, I worked with or for some of the most aggressive people in the business world, including the presidents of companies like DHL Worldwide Express, Coca-Cola, and Hormel. Those folks couldn't put saddle soap on David's muzzle.

Part of the surface charm of David is that he is a pit bull with a sense of humor. After hearing my reason for wanting to see him, he immediately put me at ease with two comments about legal malpractice that still bring a grin every time they cross my mind.

"Roger, suing lawyers is God's work."

It was one of those simple revelations that rang so true it made me want to go to law school.

"Do I really have a chance of winning against a firm like Looper, Reed?"

"It is impossible to lose a legal malpractice case."

Playing the straight man, I replied:

"How come?"

"Because no one can find twelve people who like lawyers."

Talking to David was a lot of fun.

David listened attentively to the details of Doug's membership in Eternal Values, and his mishandling of my legal affairs. He quickly told me that it would be a conflict of interest for him to take the case but that he would refer me to the best legal malpractice attorney available.

I assumed that it was just a big time put off, but within forty-eight hours I was in the office of Larry Doherty, the premier legal malpractice guy in Houston, and probably the country. From the start, Larry seemed to be marginally interested at best in my case, although he did seem to perk up when he found out that Doug had even sold gems to his own mother. We would later come to understand that Larry was consumed with a huge legal malpractice suit against Vinson & Elkins, one of Houston's silk stocking firms that had recently had an embarrassing incident involving blow jobs for their star recruits in the wine cellar of Tony's, the best restaurant in town. It was heartening to think that he was on an important mission from God, even if he was too busy to help me.

I called David back, bitched about the lack of attention, and was immediately in the office of the second best guy in town, Fritz Barnett. David seemed to have a lot of stroke.

It was during the period when we were transferring the files to Fritz that my company really began to take off with our push into the downtown Houston market. We had been selected by the administrative executive of United Gas Pipeline to handle their office lease problems, which could easily have generated several million dollars in fees over five years. He had even flown us to Dallas at his expense to meet the majority shareholder in their company.

United Gas was a very conservative organization, and my partner was terrified that the public awareness that I had been anywhere near a group as bizarre as Doug and his friends might blow the lid off the United Gas deal as well as the rest of our hard fought victories downtown. I thought he was overreacting since my butt had only been used as an exit, but he slowly convinced me to focus on money we knew we could make. He was correct in pointing out that even if you were right it was always a crap shoot expecting justice in the legal system.

There was a two-year statute of limitations on legal malpractice, and we were coming up on the second anniversary of Doug's settlement of my suit at the direction of Frederick von Mierers. So I decided to let it go.

The day after my partner and I agreed to forget the whole thing in favor of getting on with our rapidly expanding business,

David Berg called to tell me that he had entered my name as a person having relevant knowledge in the case of *Wyatt v. Sakowitz*, and that Doug's lawyer was going to depose me.

On the one hand, David had used me to a great extent to the benefit of Bobby Sakowitz. It was not my intention to get into their war. That in itself isn't really good or bad, and it certainly fits the general rule that I'm sure Doug's stepfather, Oscar Wyatt, would agree to. . .when you are in a fight, you should hit the opponent as hard as you can with absolutely anything that you can lay your hands on. In David's case, he knows extremely well just how ugly the world can be. In a *Newsweek* column he wrote at the time of John Lennon's murder, he remembered the murder of his own brother and how he found out about it by looking into the newspaper box on the way to work and seeing a picture of his brother's skull with a deputy sheriff pointing to the bullet hole in it, accompanied, of course, by the appropriately sensationalistic headlines and captions. The guy who killed his brother was acquitted, killed someone else, got out, and then killed a Federal judge. I guess that finally got the attention of the criminal justice system, and they locked him up for a while.

On the other hand, it was a chance to expose his involvement in a dangerous cult to his family and maybe shake Doug out of it so he could get some professional help. He still wasn't a bad guy himself, he was just totally controlled by a bunch of crazy Nazis from outer space.

Besides, no one but the lawyers and the principals would ever know what I said. Right? As far as I knew, David Berg had no reason to lie to me and repeatedly guaranteed that the information would be confidential.

The deposition is the topic of another story, but the day after mine was taken David called to let me know that the deposition was a matter of public record, and that some parties involved intended to make Doug's involvement in the cult front page news in every paper in the civilized world. My partner freaked. I was calm because it was clear in the deposition that the gory details had come from interviews with former members of the cult. I was recruited but had never been a member or enjoined any of their core beliefs.

An upstart weekly called *The Houston Press* ran the first story with the headline "Beam me up, Dougie." It was sensationalistic rather than investigative, and I began to get worried.

I was leaving the locker room after a workout at the Texas Club on Tuesday, August 27, 1991, and ran into Don Mason, the father of one of the kids on my tee-ball team. He was an editor at the *Houston Chronicle*, and something of a mystery to me. Our kids attended Montessori school together as well as participating in sports. Don annoyed me by virtue of his being one of those parents who was frequently too busy with work or his after hours pursuit of an M.B.A. to attend the activities of his children. The child rearing was left to his wife, a part time reporter for the *Chronicle,* and one of the nicest people I had met. Since moving downtown, I had often seen him roaming the retail areas of downtown Houston's underground, usually in the company of much younger women. This was the first time he had bothered to acknowledge my existence.

"Are you the Roger Hall in *The Houston Press* this week?"

"I'm afraid so."

"We're doing a story on Wyatt's cult. Are you talking to the press?"

"Not if I can help it."

"Well, the woman doing the story for us is really good, and you can trust her to do it right. Will you talk to her?"

Whether I liked him or not, he was alerting me to the possibility of a much larger problem. His newspaper was the most powerful in the state. A mistake there could be lethal, and the initial media coverage had been considerably less than professional.

"As long as she makes it clear that I hate these characters, and that I was a recruit rather than a member."

"She's completely honest. I'll have her call you this afternoon."

Catherine Chriss called me and seemed to be a nice lady. On Wednesday she came to my office and made it clear that she was only interested in the cult itself and that her story was going to run in the Metropolitan section of the paper, which is relatively obscure and full of local stories of strangeness anyway. I told her up front that I was not going to get crosswise with Oscar Wyatt and that any references to him would have to come straight from the deposition. She agreed, asked me a series of clarifying questions, and wanted a picture of me and my daughter for the story, since we had discussed Doug's idiocy in preaching hatred of women to the doting father of a seven-year-old girl. My wife objected, so they took a picture of me running in Memorial Park where most of Doug's recruiting effort had taken place.

Finally, someone would get it right and this thing could just go away.

* * * * *

My family and I had gone to Galveston Island south of Houston for Labor Day weekend, and we stopped at the store on Saturday afternoon to get some food for breakfast on Sunday. The *Houston Chronicle* truck had just rolled up to unload the early version of the Sunday, September 1, paper. As my wife and kids went into the store, I went to get a copy of the paper to see if they really did go to the trouble to put the cult story in the Metropolitan section on such short notice.

As I looked down at the pile, I saw my full-color picture underneath the masthead, with the page one banner headline of "A Cult of the Wealthy." The caption by my picture announced to the readership that I had been a member of the cult rather than a recruit of my lawyer and had only recently left them.

It was terrifying, but surely the people that knew me would know better.

* * * * *

Within forty-eight hours of the article, the business I had spent twelve years building was destroyed. Clients that we had worked for years to develop left us without the even the benefit of a chance to tell my side of the story. With no money coming from me, my wife was forced to resign as head resident in the pediatrics program at the University of Texas Medical School at Houston and try to immediately find a job. People who had known us for years would not let their kids play with my kids. For the first time in my life, I was forced to resort to the use of powerful antidepressant drugs administered by a psychiatrist just to get out of bed.

The city that once called me its "Outstanding Young Houstonian," as it had previously called Denton Cooley and George Bush, had become a Siberian prison for me. I had to take my name tag off at the elementary school open house. The parents at soccer practice who had scrambled to get their kids on teams that I coached were terrified of me. Old friends turned and went the other way in grocery story aisles.

Within two weeks, it was obvious that my life was

effectively destroyed. For several days, I debated the value of trying to live and rebuild the lives of my family that I had unwittingly destroyed or to simply get out of their way. My wife had a stable income for the rest of her life, and, at the time, thanks to what was soon described to me as exogenous clinical depression, I just assumed that kids have a way of recovering from anything. Shelly was also young enough and still beautiful. She could surely find someone who wouldn't screw things up on this order of magnitude to help her raise my puppies.

    I went to the safety deposit box at our bank, read the suicide section of my life insurance policy and assured myself that it was payable since it had been five years since the policy was issued. State Farm only guarded themselves against suicide for money for two years. I went to Carter's Country, our big wholesale gun dealer in Houston, and bought a Colt .380 pistol and a box of high-velocity hollow-point bullets. For about twenty minutes that afternoon, I looked in the mirror and calculated the best trajectory for a bullet through the roof of the mouth and into the brain to guarantee instant death with a minimum of disfigurement and blood loss. It was important to me, because one of my rotten jobs in college was as an orderly in a hospital. We had one poor dumb son of a bitch who had tried to blow his head off with a shotgun and had picked a bad angle. He succeeded in blowing off his chin, part of his nose, and most of one cheek. Not only did he get to live, he got to look in the mirror every morning.

The kids were laying on the floor watching TV with my wife, and I had gone into the guest bedroom, covered my head with a pillow, and was asking God to forgive me for what I was going to do. My wife had already become accustomed to my frequent retreats into the total darkness. As usual, she had been up all night at the hospital and was sound asleep. One sleeping child was snuggled into each arm.

I went back into the guest room, turned the lever to lock the door and got the Colt .380 out from under the mattress. As a single candle flickered on the dresser, I flicked off the safety as the raised sight on the end of the barrel touched the back of my throat. As I pulled the hammer back the door, which had evidently been left slightly ajar, opened and in came my very sleepy five year old son.

Quickly putting the gun under a hand towel on the sink I lay down on the guest bed. He crawled up on the foot and down to me. Settling in beside me he kissed my cheek and said:

"You are the best daddy in the whole world."

I got up, and got on with life.

The War Begins

"People seem to fight about things very unsuitable for fighting. They make a frightful noise in support of very quiet things. They knock each other about in the name of very fragile things."

C.K. Chesterton, <u>Generally Speaking</u>

"Therefore stand up and win glory; conquer your enemies and enjoy an opulent kingdom. By Me and none other have they already been slain; be an instrument only, O Arjuna."

Lord Krishna to Arjuna, <u>The Bhagavad Gita</u>

It was obvious that even though patently untrue, the Chronicle article had been understood by the business community to say that I had been a member of Eternal Values at one time, even if the decision had been made to leave. As far as my client base was concerned a former "neo-Nazi faggot from outer space" as I had come to be known on Houston's most popular morning radio show, was no better than a current one. Stone walls had immediately been built around every account and contact except for a few very close old friends. I had become a pariah.

One of my personal projects in the two years prior to September 1991 had been an effort to rebuild the life of a developer friend who had been financially devastated by the depression in Texas resulting from the collapse of oil prices. Scorpion had come from nowhere in the late 1970s to establish himself as a force to be reckoned with in Houston office building development by 1981. Time after time he humiliated established institutional developers by winning fights for big tenants. After a string of successful deals with him on behalf of my Texas clients, I invited him to bid on the national headquarters facility project for DHL Worldwide Express in San Francisco. Against incredible odds, he beat out every major suburban developer in the area and was chosen to develop DHL's facility in Redwood City, California. When it was over, DHL got a great deal, Scorpion got his break into national development, and my employer at the time, the Horne Company, got a check for $900,000.

Scorpion had also developed two beautiful buildings in Houston's western suburbs just outside what had become known as the "Energy Corridor." Already the home of giants like Conoco, Amoco, and Exxon Chemical, the area was ripe for further relocation. Every week brought the announcement that another executive had decided to escape Houston's high rental rates downtown or snarled traffic in the Galleria area by moving to the Energy Corridor.

With customary bravado, Scorpion had gone head to head with the legendary Gerald Hines in attempting to get the business of Global Marine Drilling Company, the world's largest offshore drilling contractor. When the dust settled, Hines was holding a beautifully bound proposal package, while Scorpion was heading home with the lease contract.

In a mistake common among the "bullet proof" young Texas real estate developers of the early 1980s, he had allowed his young company to expand at a staggering pace -- and his personal liability for debt to grow even faster. As with many of the high flyers of the time, the financial house of cards he had built was to collapse around him in the first ill wind.

In a series of events foreseen by no one, including Global Marine, rig utilization had slowed to the point in 1983 that Global was forced to file for Chapter 11 protection from creditors. One of the first obligations to be relieved in bankruptcy court is the office lease. After a single call from the president of Global, Scorpion was looking down the barrel of millions of dollars in personal liability for a building still occupied, but occupied by a company with no obligation to pay him rent. Scorpion struggled for five years to recover from the fiasco, but by 1988 he had been financially and emotionally pummeled into a despondent shadow of his former self. My little company continued to thrive as a result of a diversified national clientele rather than a purely oil industry client base, so I provided Scorpion with office space and support staff while he tried to pull his organization back together. By the time I made the decision to move to a prestigious location downtown in early 1991, Scorpion was helping me with deals and slowly becoming my backup with corporate contacts.

* * * * *

Our new office on the sixty-ninth floor of the tallest building in the Southwest had a breathtaking view of downtown Houston below, the Astrodome to the south, and the Galleria area to the west. We had full scale models of every major market right outside our windows. Scorpion went from looking like a refugee from Auschwitz to having a renewed interest in business.

We met with considerable initial success in our organized effort to take over the downtown office leasing market, and by September Scorpion had seen a $100,000 check with his name on it for the first time in many years. Clearly on the road to recovery, he was actually more devastated than me by the fallout from the *Chronicle* story.

When I got into the office on the Wednesday following the publication, Scorpion gave me a stack of materials on libel law, courtesy of a litigator friend of his with a law firm residing just below us in Texas Commerce Tower. As I began to read, the clouds began to settle outside my window so that the bottom half of the window was snow white and the top half perfectly blue. The only thing visible was the pinnacle of Transco Tower in the distance. I took it to be an indication of a goal in the distance. If only I had known how distant.

In less than an hour of reading, it became absolutely clear that soon workmen would be painting my likeness on the side of the Chronicle headquarters across the street from our building and changing the name from "The Houston Chronicle" to "Roger's Daily." Every single line of the chapters on defamation recovery seemed to be in my favor.

I immediately began to make a list of the good lawyers that had come into my life, most as a result of involvement in social programs over the years. The list was extensive, but my energy was already dissipating. Whatever the choice, it needed to be made quickly before I lost the ability to fight. Scorpion had insisted upon bringing his old secretary from their development company with him. I was ambivalent at first but had actually fired her at one point for coming in five hours late after a four-day holiday weekend and then throwing a fit because my call to her home woke her up. Scorpion pleaded on her behalf, and in what ultimately proved to be a major mistake I backed off and let her continue to work. She had been employed as a temporary secretary at a number of law firms after the failure of the development company, and she had a sister who had become a professional husband hunter via the route of roving legal secretary. They had a number of recommendations on potential litigators, and I was open to suggestions. I gave my notes on Doug Wyatt and Eternal Values to the sister, and she was quickly off to see a high profile friend of hers about the suit. She returned in a few hours with a comment that was my very first indication of the road ahead.

"He said if it walks like a duck, sounds like a duck, and looks like a duck -- it's a duck."

Not being prepared for a negative response to what I thought was a lawyer's dream, my response was less than eloquent.

"Huh?"

"He said it was pretty clear to him that you were in the cult."

I took the list of former cult members willing to testify under oath that I had never been a member, three pages of character references, and a long written history of public service that included massive contributions to the Anti-Defamation League back to my office to see where the evidence could be hiding that made me a duck. It was immediately obvious that none of the materials had been read. One envelope with a glue seal and clasp had not even been opened. It was the indication of a syndrome that would appear again and again. The *Houston Chronicle* played a major role in the social mobility of all who sought to make their mark in Houston. My real opponent in litigation, the wealthy and powerful Hearst corporation, would be tough to beat even if the playing field was even. From the beginning it was obvious that for the financially successful personal injury lawyers who had plenty of slam dunk car wreck suits to handle, it was far easier to just agree with the radio guys that I was a Nazi faggot from outer space.

Seeing little sense in further pursuit of strangers, I made my first personal call to Aubrey Calvin. I had met Aubrey on a public service call and quickly decided to ask him to join the Board of Directors of my Drug Free Business Initiative. He was a physically slight, nervously intelligent man who reminded me of the space physics people I used to meet on the steps of the graduate student bar at Rice University. When the "Valhalla" crowd talked about farming the asteroid belt they were serious, and I was hoping to find an attorney from that intellectual neighborhood.

Aubrey quickly invited me over to the offices of Calvin, Dylewski, Gibbs, & Mattox on the forty-fifth floor of First Interstate Tower. He was the only guy I had met in the Republican stronghold of Houston who had the guts to hang pictures of John Kennedy all over his walls.

Aubrey's pursuit of all relevant facts led to a discussion of the *Chronicle's* motivation for making a seemingly obscure story into front page material. I told him that I had learned about the *Chronicle's* hatred of Doug's stepfather Oscar Wyatt from a man close to the families (hereinafter known as "Cobra"), which he already knew. Then I mentioned Cobra's influence.

Aubrey exploded.

"Cobra! What's that son of a bitch got to do with the paper?"

"You know him?"

I had hit a sore spot far beyond my expectations.

"Everybody knows him. He has done more for the cocaine trade than Pablo Escobar."

I was generally aware that Cobra had a colorful reputation, but did not know any real specifics about his past.

"How?"

"He has contacts throughout the world in the organized drug trade. You need to be very careful with Cobra. He has dirt files on every top law enforcement officer and prosecutor in town."

I continued to believe at that point that Cobra was okay and that Aubrey probably just had battle scars that were surfacing. On the other hand, Aubrey was as guarded and unemotional as they came. It was not at all like him to make a strong statement about anyone unless he was convinced of his ability to back it up.

We talked more as Aubrey employed his Socratic method of determining if I was holding some dark secret that might surface down the road to color his having referred me to a friend. When comfortable that there were no Nazi skeletons in my closet, he finally committed to a name.

"You need to call Wayne Paris. Wayne was a prosecutor with the U.S. Attorney's office for years and has gone into private practice. He's completely honest and should have no love loss for the *Chronicle*. I'll call him to give you an introduction."

After making my way through the air-conditioned tunnel system that keeps the corporate carpenter ants of Houston from soaking their wool suits with sweat in the constant hundred degree heat of September, I rode the escalator up to the main lobby of Texas Commerce Tower. As the mammoth door opened that would take me and seventy others to the sixtieth floor observation area for transfer to the penthouse area, an old friend (now a competitor) from my days at the Horne Company emerged with a client. He spotted me and immediately shouted:

"A celebrity! That's a tough way to get your picture on the front page of the paper, Rog."

It was obvious that the topic of conversation for the rest of the walk with his client would be about how careful an executive had to be when choosing a broker to handle millions of dollars of a company's money. Even the most seasoned corporate soldier could make a fatal career move if he unwittingly chose the "wrong" kind of guy.

I got off on the sixty-ninth floor, went straight to my office, and called for an appointment with Wayne Paris.

* * * * *

The damage to my business continued to grow

exponentially, and my mental condition was going straight to hell. My largest and best client for many years had been Coca-Cola Foods, a $3 billion division of The Coca-Cola Company, best known for its Minute Maid products. From the beginning, my contact at Coca-Cola had been Matt Miller, who proved to be the kindest and most honest man I had ever known. A series of odd events inside Coke had resulted in Matt taking the number two position in a coffee company sold by Coca-Cola to a private investor. Less than eight months after the sale, the company was sold again -- this time to Procter & Gamble.

Matt had plenty of other things to worry about, but went out of his way to support me during the period following the article. For thirty years Matt's secretary had been Nancy Red. I was absolutely certain that Nancy was my friend, and that she could not possibly harbor any question about my integrity. One of my most poignant moments in learning the incredible power of the press came during a phone call the day before my scheduled meeting with Wayne Paris. I had called Matt to get his opinion on lawyers before committing to a representative. He was out of town, and Nancy answered:

"Mr. Miller's office."

One of the old fashioned but charming things about their relationship was that even after thirty years and God knows how many personal and professional crises they had weathered together, she still addressed him as "Mr. Miller."

"Nancy, it's Roger."

"Boy oh boy, are we getting a lot of calls about you."

"It's the high price of free speech, Nancy."

I was not up to humor, but sarcasm was still easy.

"I've had so many people come in here and ask 'Is Roger Hall really a homosexual?' I tell them that if he is, I'll just quit."

Nancy, my buddy of eleven years, had just told me that she was not sure of my sexual preference. The obvious implication was that she was not convinced of my real nature in any regard. Daggers to the heart come in all shapes and sizes. This one was the size of a Volkswagen bus, and honed to a razor-sharp edge.

If eleven years of friendship, albeit professionally distant in Nancy's case, could not insulate me against uncertainty, what would? For years I had held multiple secrets about Coca-Cola in confidence, including some that would blow their squeaky clean public image to Hell. Matt Miller was the ultimate corporate executive. He had never even implied a single negative thing about anyone in all our years together. But in all my travels on behalf of Coca-Cola, there had been plenty of other managers and employees that were not so blindly loyal and guarded. The idea that Coca-Cola would be rampant with rumors about me for reports of behavior they knew were untrue really hurt. I just hung up the phone.

Having lost all energy again, I decided to focus on the clean up of company financial matters. We had a great deal of cash on hand by our standards and more coming in. Even though the vast majority of our work for clients was accomplished using local brokers who worked for commissions I had a monthly overhead of fifteen thousand dollars for only three full-time employees. It would not take long to drain the coffers if our pipeline of potential revenue continued to evaporate.

Scorpion had gone to lunch, so I went into his office and extracted the files with bills, outstanding invoices, and revenue projections. Every businessman has his weak spots, and attention to financial detail was clearly one of mine. My wife and our CPA, Nick Endres, cringed at the very thought of having to take my records at the end of the year for preparation of tax reports. But from the first year of operation, they had invariably found that I had overpaid taxes. It was annoying to them, and arguably stupid in light of the zero rate of interest offered by the Internal Revenue Service for overpayment, but the bottom line always showed the same thing -- overpaid taxes.

Superficially this syndrome was the expression of a poor kid's attitude about debt. My wife and I had never been a single day late on any payment of any kind from the time we moved into our ten by fifty foot trailer in Joplin, Missouri, to the day we moved into our four thousand foot brick monster in one of Houston's most affluent neighborhoods. But the issue was considerably deeper. I was absolutely terrified of the Internal Revenue Service. Nick Endres had been with the IRS for many years before joining a firm in private practice, and his experiences coupled with my own eyewitness view of those that had incurred the wrath of our only unrestrained government agency fueled the paranoia. I had personally seen IRS agents and local police armed with shotguns, chains, and padlocks enter a building in suburban Houston to shut a company down for tax problems. Scorpion had been reduced to shivering human Jello by the agents negotiating his payment schedule.

From the very start of our association, Scorpion had insisted on handling the books. My wife had wanted to apply her German sense of order to the process for years, but I thought that juggling medical school and motherhood was plenty for her to handle. The decision to let Scorpion take over was easy, as long as I signed most of the checks. His only specific instructions from me were to never, under any circumstance whatsoever, get me anywhere near a conflict with the IRS. This instruction was repeated at least weekly throughout our affiliation.

Before long, and for God knows what reason we had a Packard Bell computer operating under DOS, a new accounting system, automated checks, and a service to handle our tax reporting. It was a pain in the ass since my expertise was in the use of Macintosh computers and software, but I had bigger fish to fry.

The month of August had been a slow one for cash flow, but there was plenty coming in for September and the rest of 1991. This knowledge, coupled with positive initial response to our new marketing program made it relatively easy for me to agree with Scorpion's request in August for a new company car and a cash advance -- even though he had yet to turn up a single piece of business on his own. Through all his trouble, Scorpion had held onto his home in River Oaks, Houston's most expensive neighborhood, and his kids still went to a private school with tuition only slightly below that of Harvard. My wife had often commented on this somewhat twisted set of priorities from a man who was under the gun of the federal government for a huge personal debt, but I understood the frail and illogical nature of the developer ego. Scorpion was going need a full recovery of his once mammoth ego to score the big commission hits it was going to take to bail himself out. He was not going to survive by cutting a few thousand dollars a month from his lifestyle.

Tucked under a stack of otherwise meaningless paper in the back of the accounts payable file were two notices from my CPA that we were risking serious trouble with the IRS for nonpayment of taxes from the first quarter, and that penalties and interest were rapidly mounting. I was stunned. The reports I had just been given from Scorpion's newpayroll service and the second quarter tax report (signed by Scorpion) both indicated that we had no outstanding tax liability. I called Nick and learned that he had simply failed to call me due to assurances from Scorpion that I knew of the problem. Nick had even ignored a written query from me about my personal tax status as a result of company activity because Scorpion had told him that he had personally prepared a report for me after being given a copy of my letter to Nick by "our" secretary -- even though he was not to have been copied on it.

For a brief moment, my depression turned to fury. Where the hell did the money from our checking account go if it did not go to the IRS? I knew from experience that Scorpion could tell you where the nickels had gone from his first allowance as a child, so it was not a matter of accidental and honest misplacement. And why did he fail to tell me about thousands of dollars in mounting penalties and interest? As a Subchapter S corporation, I was individually liable -- and he knew it.

I went back in to examine the top of his desk with its multiple neat piles of documents, and discovered the larger answer to my question. Scorpion had mentioned to me his having some trouble with Houston's largest title company, Stewart Title. I never listened to the details of the story because I figured his personal financial business was his and mine was mine. It also seemed that every time I listened to another hard luck story it cost me more money.

A document prepared by Stewart Title had been opened to a paragraph that he had been working on during the morning. The paragraph was a written admission that Scorpion had been guilty of criminal fraud in a transaction with Stewart, but they were agreeing to forego pursuit of criminal prosecution if he would make them a secured creditor second only to the IRS for repayment. Knowing that Scorpion's old schoolmate and buddy was the president of Stewart, it was clear that this was an act of mercy. The details documented in the following pages would have been a dream come true for an assistant district attorney looking for a white collar bust.

I hated cliches, and I hated television commercials even more, but the Morton salt "When it rains, it pours" slogan came to mind and would not leave.

I went home and went through all the records twice just to be sure. Scorpion was brilliant. He had made millions of dollars building office buildings. In his spare time he had renovated a classic Houston bank building and turned it into one of the premier night clubs in Texas, featuring acts like B.B. King, the Four Tops, Stevie Ray Vaughn, and The Fabulous Thunderbirds. Now it was clear that he was as self-serving as he was intelligent.

It would be a year later before I would tell him in writing that he was a snake, but the message God was sending me about the fleeting and shallow nature of relationships built around money was loud and clear. Scorpion was an atheist, an aspect of his cosmogony that had always concerned me, but then I was no washed in the blood of the lamb saint either. But in all the years and through all the deals, I had not ever lied to a client or even considered stealing. This was the final straw.

My first reaction after verifying the betrayal was to fire him. In a faint-hearted attempt, I called the office and told him to get all of his files ready for me to review.

Going up the elevator to the observation floor was never my favorite ride, and today it was tantamount to torture. Fear of being recognized was not a good state of mind for a marketing guy, and the pulsating ocean of slick young MBAs and lawyers was making me seasick.

When the door opened, I rushed out and physically ran into the top administrative officer of United Gas Pipeline, Gayle Wilke. Gayle was a nice man but more than a bit unsettled by the pressure of downsizing his company in the continued decline of the oil business. He and I had met several times about our working for him, and he had gone so far as to fly Scorpion and me to Dallas at his expense to meet United's majority shareholders and introduce us as his recommendation for their representatives in the renegotiation of their 300,000 square foot office lease. It was going to be our first grand slam home run in the downtown market, and we had whipped every major brokerage firm in Houston to get the deal, even though my involvement in Houston real estate had been limited for many years. We were negotiating the contract with United when the article appeared, and getting it signed would have guaranteed us at least $1.2 million in new fees over the next year.

Gayle had not returned the call I had made to him. The look on his face explained why. It was not a look of hate or disbelief but one of sadness and betrayal. He was a fundamentalist Christian, and one of the most conservative people I had ever known. His own position in United Gas was very shaky -- not because of his personal performance, but simply because high-priced administrative people are always among the first to go when a big company focuses on cost cutting. He was in no position to support anyone with the baggage carried by me.

We walked quietly to the thirty-foot-high glass wall looking into downtown. One of the never-ending bus loads of elementary school children inched slowly and fearfully to the curtain wall for a peek off the side of Houston's only accessible mountain peak.

"How are you holding up, Roger?"

"It's okay, Gayle. I've been told it's a great libel suit, and I'm going to see a lawyer on Thursday."

"My wife and I are praying for you."

He meant it, and I suddenly felt tears begin to well in my eyes.

"You're a good man, Gayle. How's your deal going?"

"There is no honor or integrity anymore, Roger."

"Final days?"

"I believe so."

We walked back toward the elevator, shook hands, and he disappeared in one of the continual waves of Gucci surf. We never spoke again.

Scorpion was waiting at his desk. He always looked to be much younger than his forty-two years, but today he looked like a terrified teenager. Every single file he had lay on the desk. He was shivering.

He started in on one of his professionally curt lines of intellectual bullshit, which were normally annoying but today unbearable. I stopped him in the middle of a sentence, and he shattered like a crystal vase landing on a granite floor.

"You knew that not fucking with the IRS was my only rule."

"It all got confused because of the transfer to the agency."

"Scorpion, you're the only person I know who can tell you within ten cents what he has spent in the last two years. You can do detailed drawings of the inside of a night club on a cocktail napkin, and estimate the build-out cost of an entire building a year before construction. Do you really expect me to sit here and believe that you woke up with twenty thousand dollars more in your checking account one morning than you were supposed to have and didn't bother to find out why."

"It's the truth."

"Then why didn't you show me the notices from Nick saying that the shit had hit the fan and was heading toward me."

"I was afraid you'd be angry..."

"No joke, Scorpion. After all the things we've been through and done together. Where are you going to find another broker to give you a hundred thousand dollar gift to get your feet back on the ground?"

He was battered and incapable of fighting. I was trembling with rage.

"Scorpion, do you remember when we moved in up here, and you asked 'Is this heaven?'"

"Yeah."

"And do you remember telling me that not many boys from Joplin, Missouri, get to the sixty-ninth floor of Texas Commerce Tower?"

"Sure."

"Well this ain't heaven, and the only boy from Joplin, Missouri, that made it wishes to God he hadn't."

I walked out of his office. He stayed on through the roll down of the company, and our relationship quickly deteriorated to mutual loathing.

We would close a few more deals that were outstanding and unravel our contractual obligations. Scorpion's overt expression of hatred is curtness and mine is avoidance. We spoke little even during the evening when ten years of my records were filed for the last time in a dumpster borrowed from the building management. We had once told each other things we would not tell our wives, children, or bartenders. Now we couldn't even tell each other goodbye.

I tried to believe the story I often repeated when someone who knew of the break up would ask about details. My response was always:

"There are two kind of dogs that will bite you. Bad dogs, and good dogs that are wounded. Either way you're bit, but you take the good dogs to the vet and shoot the bad dogs." I will never know for sure which kind of dog Scorpion was deep down inside, but a slip from the attorney for the *Chronicle* would soon come to give me a pretty good idea.

* * * * *

In order to complete my near perfect day after confronting Scorpion, I had to return a few phone calls. One was from an attorney we had used for preparation of a variety of corporate documents and once on a collection problem. Coachwhip was a real estate and tax attorney, and we had once officed in the same building near my former home in Bellaire -- an incorporated oasis surrounded on all sides by the city of Houston. Bellaire is known for large lots, oak trees, and a gestapo-style police force, which served to keep Bellaire's crime rate far below that of its bigger neighbor.

Coachwhip's receptionist did not recognize my voice, which was good. Neither did his secretary. At least I could make a phone call without fear.

"Coachwhip."

"Hey, Coachwhip, it's Roger Hall."

"You're famous!"

"Can you believe this?"

Coachwhip knew of my involvement in a number of public service activities and was not likely to believe I was secretly getting buttfucked by reincarnated aliens and hanging out with Nazi woman haters as I waited for the spaceships to arrive.

"Are you going to sue them?"

"One of Scorpion's girlfriends is a litigator at McConn & Hardy. She gave him a stack of materials that make me believe that they have a big problem."

"How did it happen?"

"One of the parents on my tee ball team set me up. Don Mason is a manager at the *Chronicle* and he told me this woman could absolutely be trusted, and they were going to do a story no matter what, so I would do well to make sure she got it right."

"Assassinated by a tee ball parent."

"It's a funny world, Coachwhip."

He didn't call to talk about my problems. I had involved Coachwhip in a fee dispute that had pitted him against a vicious Manhattan attorney representing a developer who owed me money. Lurking just below the good old boy exterior in Coachwhip was a pit bull who measured his productive time in seconds rather than pieces of hours like most lawyers.

"You need to come and see us."

"I've got plenty of trouble, but none of it is collection trouble."

"No, you need to come and see us about the libel suit. I just hired an old buddy from law school. He's one of the best First Amendment guys in the country."

"Who is he?"

"Cottonmouth -- he's been with the ACLU for years and is finally tired of starving. He's going to do all kinds of personal injury litigation for me, but his real expertise is in defamation."

"Well, I've got an appointment with Aubrey Calvin's guy."

"Come and see us first."

"When?"

"Right now."

I needed to get the lawyer issue resolved one way or the other. My depression had begun to express itself as lethargy, and had obviously been compounded by learning of Scorpion's betrayal. I needed assistance in any event, and having an offer from Coachwhip's guy might be handy if only to negotiate with Wayne Paris about fees.

"Give me about forty-five minutes."

It was one more ride down from the clouds and into the parking garage. Something other than simple fatigue was going on inside me, but I had no clue yet that it was clinical depression. The hundreds of people I passed in the underground area of the tower seemed to be speaking a foreign language, and they shuffled along in slow motion like so many cattle being invisibly herded from holding pens to the slaughterhouse.

The drive to Coachwhip's office in the suburbs took me down I-59 past the Summit where the trouble had all begun over a pair of Rockets tickets. Behind the Summit were the twin towers of silver glass housing Doug's law firm and daddy's Coastal Corporation. I wondered how Doug was holding up under the pressure of the trial, the awful publicity, and what had to be some intense scrutiny from his homophobic father. But then he might have avoided it all by refusing to rip off his friends for his guru. . .

The freeway quickly connected with Loop 610, Houston's innermost traffic circle. What had to be the area's premier billboard rose in the intersection of the two heavily traveled arteries. It shouted "Erase Illiteracy" and was sponsored by the *Houston Chronicle*. Good idea, learn to read so you can have your mind filled with senseless horseshit like everyone else.

One of the advantages of Coachwhip's location was that unlike downtown, visitors could park directly in front of the back door. I made the short walk down the ceramic tile hallway to a real human sized elevator, instead of the percolating basketball courts of Texas Commerce.

Downtown lawyers in Houston referred to those not downtown as "Loop Lawyers" or those in the "Hinterlands," both condescending references indicating inability or unwillingness to support the overhead associated with a prestigious downtown location. Coming back to the quiet suburban building made me wonder why I had ever gone downtown at all.

The receptionist jumped to her feet and quickly shuffled me into a conference room at the end of the building facing the

Astrodome. I took a seat with my back to the window and started thinking through my answers to the obvious questions that were coming. Before I could begin, Coachwhip, his partner Diamondback, and a slightly heavy and disheveled dark-haired man, obviously Cottonmouth, entered the room. We dispensed quickly with introductions, and Cottonmouth took charge by asking me a series of questions. He seemed to be most interested in the reporter's promise that she would make it clear in the article that I had never been more than an unwitting recruit of the cult -- not a member. He would later explain that the only libel cases upheld by the U.S. Supreme Court in recent times had been breach of contract cases. I took his educational lecture to indicate that he was willing to go as far as necessary to win -- a good initial sign.

After sufficient assemblage of the relevant facts, Cottonmouth summarized first his view of the suit:

"I just wanted to see what the jury was going to think of you, and they're going to love you. But you need to understand that the law is not on your side. Libel is almost impossible to win. This could take years, and you could end up losing on the last day."

"What did you think of the article?" I was still hoping someone would tell me it wasn't that bad.

"I called my wife to tell her we were meeting. She couldn't remember you until I mentioned the picture of you running. Then she said 'Oh, you mean Dougie's boyfriend.'"

It was not exactly the reassurance I was hoping for.

Coachwhip then began the marketing charge.

"We want to represent you. It won't cost you a thing. We get a third of any judgment or settlement, and we pay all expenses."

My one previous experience in litigation had also been as plaintiff and had sensitized me to the enormous amounts of money the legal system can extract in the form of expenses even if you are supposed to be working with your lawyer on a purely contingent fee basis. He had gotten my attention.

But years of being misled by business people had made me aware that any deal that sounded too good to be true probably was.

"Well, if these suits are so hard to win, why do you want to take this one so much?"

Cottonmouth jumped in to respond.

"The *Chronicle* has two reasons to be afraid of you. One is that you are clearly a private rather than a public figure. The law is still bad from your perspective, but more favorable to you than a politician or other public person. But their main problem is the size of your actual damages. The appellate courts are vicious when it comes to disallowing punitive damages, but actual damages have a far better chance of being upheld."

"So how do we figure those?"

"Take your average income for the last five years, and multiply it by the number of years that you would have had to work until sixty-five if they had not destroyed your business."

A brief moment of mental arithmetic gave me a figure of about fifteen million dollars. My guess was that five million dollar fees were pretty rare for small real estate and tax firms. And the ACLU probably did not send out a lot of million dollar checks to its lawyers either.

Diamondback broke the short silence.

"And the punitive damages have no limit."

Suddenly I saw the light of their interest.

"What do we ask for?"

Coachwhip wanted to answer that one.

"We ask the jury to send a message to the Hearst Corporation that they cannot avoid understanding."

"Such as?"

"Figure the liquidated value of the Chronicle is $350 million."

I was not yet in a warlike state of mind, mainly because the pain was still too intense, but even at this point it was perfectly logical for me to think that if the paper made this magnitude of mistake, they should expect a big hit.

Coachwhip's offer still seemed too good to be true, especially given their willingness to have the firm foot the bill on all expenses. The expenses were an unknown and possibly very large number, and my short-term financial future was about as solid as a marriage to Elizabeth Taylor. I was a big fan of any deal where the people working for me only make money if I make money. But the contract was yet to be seen. Dealing with landlords in places like Long Island City had given me a deep awareness that the deal you hear is not always the deal you read.

"I need to look at your agreement."

Coachwhip jumped to his feet, and returned quickly from his office with a brief three-page document. To my amazement, the contract was even cleaner than the conversation -- all the way down to my unilateral option to fire them for "any reason or for no reason" at any time with an obligation to reimburse them only for actual out of pocket costs and fees for their time, and then only if there was a settlement or award. Either they believed it was a hell of a suit or they had a great show.

I finished reading and tried not to sound or look impressed.

"It's pretty clean, but the word 'reasonable' needs to be inserted in here before 'fees and costs' for purposes of clarity."

I said clarity, but they understood that I meant taking their girlfriend to the Bahamas in order to alleviate stress before trial was not going in the hopper. Coachwhip jumped to his feet again and was back in less than ten minutes with the revision.

"Are we ready to sign it?"

"I've got a meeting with Wayne Paris tomorrow. . ."

"This is a today deal." Coachwhip was pushing.

If there was any rule of business I had learned over the years it was that when anyone for any reason is pushing you to sign something quickly, it is inevitably better for them than you;

regardless of how it may seem at the time they are pushing. In what would ultimately prove to be an act of unadulterated nescience I broke from my historical wall of resistance to sales pressure and signed their deal.

I was weak, tired, and depressed. Excerpts from my psychological diary "353 Letters I Didn't Send" during this period indicate a desire for someone to step into the ring before I collapsed. It was a decision that made sense. . .in the room. . .at the time.

Cottonmouth and I talked more, and he ended with the promise of a draft demand letter for the Chronicle within twenty-four hours.

My life was going to hell, I was running out of money fast, and I really was not any of the things they said. I asked him how long it would be before we could demand a trial.

"It could be years."

The guns were being loaded and the tortoises saddled.

* * * * *

I have often heard that the two happiest days in the life of any sailboat owner are the day he gets the boat and the day he gets rid of it. This aphorism applies equally as well to lawsuits.

As mentioned earlier, my only other experience in litigation had been suing a developer for a commission on a long and arduous deal I put together at Los Angeles

International Airport. The thrill of filing suit, armed with the power of righteous indignation, against a renegade runt who refused to honor an iron clad written contract to pay me on a deal that made him a wealthy man was soon replaced by dumbfounded disbelief as his lawyers repeatedly defeated provisions of the contract with technicalities of law. I knew very well why the gray-haired members of the business community always said, "The only ones that make money in court are the lawyers."

But hope springs eternal, doesn't it? I was convinced from day one that my war with the *Chronicle* was so one-sided that the defense would quickly fold up their tent, apologize for the tragic mistake, pay up, and apply the lesson learned by becoming more responsible journalists.

Instead they told us what Professor Lucas Powe of the University of Texas School of Law reports that every libel plaintiff hears from a media defendant. Quoting the Professor: "Fuck you. You're full of shit."

The lead attorney for the Hearst Corporation, parent of the *Houston Chronicle*, was Hog-nose, respected member of a 'silk stocking' firm that also had its offices in Texas Commerce Tower. They had a reputation for vicious representation of their big clients, and the Hearst Corporation represented a very big meal ticket indeed. Following the mandatory thirty-day waiting period before filing after receipt of the demand letter for fourteen million dollars, we filed with the district court system of Texas.

My suit could have been filed in federal court since Hearst was engaged in interstate activity, but Cottonmouth felt that our chances were much better with a twelve person jury of local Texans than in the federal court system filled with judges he referred to as "Reagan and Bush appointed pawns of big business."

My initial reaction to his choice of battlefields was that although Cottonmouth was theoretically correct, the local judges might be too deeply influenced in their political careers by endorsements from the *Houston Chronicle* to give us a fair chance. Having just seen a famous family law judge go to prison for unilaterally overturning the jury verdict in *Wyatt v. Sakowitz* for what was discovered to be a bribe, I was already leery of judicial quality.

Compounding my fear of the district court system was knowledge that although the Houston Bar association compiled a ranking of the various judges according to fairness and impartiality based upon the experiences of their membership, most of the nonlegal community depended upon newspapers for recommendations on judicial races. On election day a list of politicians recommended by the *Chronicle* management was prominently displayed, and many times I had seen people reading the *Chronicle's* list while waiting to vote. Although your average Texan might know the story on major races, contests for positions like judge of the 152nd District Court were not hot topics. Most of those endorsed by the *Chronicle* on election day won.

At face value the idea of electing judges struck me as insane. Knowing what we all knew about the dearth of ethical and moral standards in the political process, how could any state submit its constituency to dependence on judges emerging from the same process that had produced Lyndon Johnson, Jim Wright, and Bill Clements?

Once again I would ultimately learn that the most paranoid of my trepidations were lurking just ahead in painful, lucid reality.

* * * * *

In what I should have recognized as a small time lawyer seeking to enter the big time on the shoulders of my trouble, Coachwhip insisted upon issuing a press release announcing the suit. After all the headlines associated with the feral rivalry of *Wyatt v. Sakowitz*, the filing of my suit got one small paragraph in the back pages of *The Houston Post*, and a blip in the infantile *Houston Press*. Having anticipated greater coverage of a massive libel suit from the arch-rival of the *Chronicle*, Cottonmouth rationalized the puny response to their announcement as the result of the *Chronicle's* reporter that we were suing living with the managing editor of the *Post*.

Cottonmouth's insight into the sexual lives of the parties was my first indication of his long history with the local media.

As an attorney for the ACLU he had frequently dealt with reporters, but his relationship would prove to be far more complex than just professional interaction.

Cottonmouth and I spent a considerable amount of time together in the beginning, and it seemed that Coachwhip's claim of Cottonmouth having been the student law school professors always turned to when no one else knew the answer was probably true. He was exceptionally quick, and had a surly combativeness lurking just below the surface. Cottonmouth appeared to be Jewish, which I thought was great considering that part of our efforts would involve greater exposure of a group of neo-Nazis. Unfortunately, when our conversation finally turned to personal beliefs he shared ideas with me that were deeply disturbing.

One morning when we were reviewing my involvement with Eternal Values, Cottonmouth was ferociously probing for weak spots in my story. He was certain that the defense would claim that although I was not a member of the cult as the story indicated, I was close enough for them to have made an honest (and nonpunishable) error.

"Why should a jury believe you were just curious?"

"Because I have been curious about God and religion my whole life?"

"As evidenced by?"

"I was a preacher for the Church of Christ at fourteen years old for congregations in Kansas and Missouri that were too small to afford a full-time minister. I've been continually involved in sampling the doctrine of everything from Transcendental Meditation to Judaism. I've been trying to figure out the meaning of life since I was five."

"And that led you to Frederick."

"That led me to read the books and listen to the tapes Doug gave me. Come on, Cottonmouth, don't most people have a history of existential curiosity?"

"No. Most people have no curiosity at all."

"How about you, though?"

"I have a great deal of difficulty thinking that some almighty power has absolute control of my life."

"You're an atheist?"

"You're like my first wife -- constantly interrupting me mid-thought."

His first wife was a pediatrician, and on the faculty of my wife's medical school. He hated her with a passion. Her sister was a manager with the *Houston Chronicle*. He liked her even less.

"Sorry."

For the first time he gave me a look into the rigidity of his disbelief.

"Let me put it this way. My current wife once had a stroke. She was literally blind for a while, and when the stroke occurred she was in bad enough shape that a Catholic priest was called in to deliver last rights since they didn't know her religious preference. She stirred enough when he started to say 'Keep it for someone that believes your hocus pocus, father'."

It became apparent to me that I harbored at least one blanket opinion of a group of people. I was sincerely uncomfortable with those that did not believe in God at all. All my life I had believed that atheists invariably broke down on their death beds to ask for forgiveness and help. Cottonmouth and his wife were cold and profoundly nonspiritual. He was proud of the last rights story, and at least equally convicted in his own denial of any consciousness higher than that of those graduating from the University of Texas School of Law.

I was always wary of atheists, and the recent experience with Scorpion had confirmed my theory that people who answer to nothing but the laws of a material world have very few limits on their behavior. Every decision for them must be weighed in light of the probable benefit of acting as they choose as opposed to the potential loss resulting from being caught. Now I had learned that my representative in the most important fight of my life came from the same school of thought as the man who stole from me after I pulled him from the ditch. This revelation about Cottonmouth brought on an attack of buyer's remorse, but it was a bit late to be changing horses. . . especially since most of my days were now spent in bed with the covers pulled over my head.

* * * * *

As the days turned into weeks and months I became progressively more wearied by the insanity of the legal system. I had never gotten to the point of depositions and interrogatories in my only other suit, and the never ending stream of paper, response to paper, and response to response to paper was maddening. Long ago a manager at Coca-Cola Foods had told me that they dealt with suits like the one they were facing over pollution of Florida lakes with effluent from the juice-making process not by attacking the plaintiff, but by wearing them out.

"We just run up legal fees until they go away."

His comment troubled me at the time, but actually being the mouse under the paw of a three-hundred-pound cat was more than just disheartening. The eyewitness view of legal process led me to understand the absurd extent of privilege granted the wealthy in a system originally designed to provide justice for all. Those with the most money for legal fees are entitled to the most justice.

A few months into the process I received a summons for jury duty during a time when my mental state was best characterized by constant paranoid fear of being recognized. After sitting in a large auditorium for three hours, my group was finally called for interview in a criminal forgery case. A terrified young black woman squirmed behind a public defender fresh from the turnip truck as the judge gave us a speech on the responsibility of being a juror in a case that could take the freedom away from a human being. When he was done, the prosecutor from the district attorney's office began her questioning of potential jurors. It was not long before I decided that if reincarnation were in fact real this woman had been the commandant of a Nazi extermination facility in her last trip to this planet. She was overtly ruthless in her demeanor and choice of language concerning the "low life few that have no respect for the economic welfare of others."

As the afternoon progressed, the story emerged of a woman writing hot checks only to grocery stores and only for food to feed her three small children. I had often gone for walks downtown to get away from my expensive concrete cell, and one day I had been approached by a woman almost identical to the defendant. She begged me for money to feed her kids who she said were staying at a nearby mission. Her welfare check that came on the first of the month was a week away, and she was completely out of baby food and diapers. The mission was short of funding, and her kids cried at night because they were still hungry after the meager meals provided.

I had seen too many junkies with good stories to fall for it, and had become even more calloused by my frequent trips to the Children's Home to see the little ones with AIDS who were continually being retrieved from abandoned warehouse floors and alleys after mom got high and forgot that she had children.

Something was different about this woman, so instead of walking away, I looked her straight in the eye and said:

"If you want to go to the grocery store I'll go with you and pay for the food, but you are not getting any cash for crack."

She assured me she was not an addict and led me to a grocery store on the outskirts of Houston's northernmost area of downtown where she filled a cart with disposable diapers, fresh fruit, peanut butter, whole wheat bread, and microwavable entrees. I just trailed behind her and watched as a mother doing the best she could for her family did her work. She had a look that asked "Is this too much?" when approaching the checkout stand, and it would have been fruitless to explain that the hundred dollars could instead have been spent on only one lunch at a private club for myself and two clients. After she talked the manager into letting her borrow the cart by giving him the phone number of the mission a few blocks away, I walked outside with her.

"Do you need me to walk you home?"

"I'm okay. It's daytime."

As I turned to go back to the palace she said: "God bless you."

Without even turning around for fear of seeing the real world again, I told her:

"No. God needs to be spending his time taking care of good mothers like you."

When the "Hell Bitch" as I had nicknamed her after McCall's horse in *Lonesome Dove* got to me, her first question was whether it would be possible for me to send this woman accused of feeding her family to prison if found guilty.

For one moment, the depression left and the renegade returned.

"You crazy assholes in the D.A.'s office let people like Doug Wyatt get away with white collar crime every day. . .and they end up screwing common people out of millions of dollars so they can throw more parties for more rich friends, and they can sit around talking about how exquisite the fucking shaved ice desserts are. . .and you would rather trample the poor than have to think. If you expect me to send this woman to prison, you're out of your fucking mind."

The room fell silent, and I wondered if saying "fuck" in a courtroom was going to get me the night in jail. The Hell Bitch said nothing and went quietly on to the next prospect.

I was not selected for jury duty.

The ugly truth was that the same lawyer-infested jungle preying upon the forgery defendant was starting to strangle me. I was running out of money, and although the one brush with suicide had passed being out of money was very hard for me. While Hog-nose profited from the hourly fees of the *Chronicle's* defamation defense -- a line of work called "Defense Lawyer's Santa Claus" -- by legal experts, I could only watch as every conceivable legal maneuver was executed to generate fees and avoid admitting a mistake.

Little did I know that this was only the beginning of my revulsion. Before it was over I would have conclusive evidence that, at least in Texas, sections of the legal system are sometimes run of the criminals, by the criminals, and for the criminals. I would come to believe that the legal system is destroying the greatest country in the history of mankind. I would ultimately subscribe to a theory that lawyers are now predominantly parasites in the body of American society -- creating nothing, producing nothing, only taking some or all of what the productive members produce.

But for now all I could afford to believe was that we would have to escape the economic and emotional shackles of Houston in order to survive. We had once driven all night after visiting Shelly's father in Missouri after a heart attack for fear that our second child and only son would not have the privilege bestowed his sister. . .being a native Texan. Now we were slowly being forced into exile.

You Went To Prison For What?

"Commit a crime, and the earth is made of glass. There is no such thing as concealment."

Ralph Waldo Emerson, <u>Essays: First Series</u>

"Ambition often puts men upon doing the meanest offices; so climbing is performed in the same posture with creeping."

Jonathan Swift, <u>Thoughts of Various Subjects</u>

As the devastation continued it became necessary for me to take a simple action that would hurt a lot. One of our first tasks after moving to Houston in 1978 was to get an insurance agent. Shelly's family had always used State Farm, and our auto policy was with them already. At a time when our combined income was $180 per month, and we were living in a run down apartment complex next door to eleven Iranian students I happened to call a local agent named Susan Quick. Susan treated us like the most important people in the world even though we were broke, and had no hope of getting over it for a long time. By 1991 we had two cars, a boat, investment resort properties, a $400,000 house, life insurance, disability plans, and a major umbrella policy with Susan. Sometimes treating poor people with respect pays off. In fact, when we discovered that Susan's husband, Bob Goldstein, was the leasing manager for one of Texas' most successful Chrysler/Plymouth dealerships, we refused to do car deals through anyone but him whether the car was a Chrysler product or not.

Over the years they had become very close friends as well as service providers. Bob was one of the most insightful people we knew, and Susan had a sense of humor that was second to none.

They were intelligent and sensitive. They were my friends. They were Jewish. Now I had to go to Bob for help in the wake of the *Houston Chronicle's* banner headline announcement of my involvement in an international neo-Nazi group intent upon carrying through with Adolph Hitler's dreams.

It had been twelve days since the article appeared when I called Bob. I was nearly out of energy already and any resistance on his part was going to be devastating. He answered his direct line on the first ring.

"Bob here."

"Bob, it's Roger Hall."

"Roger, are you okay. We've been worried sick about you."

From the tone of his voice there was no question that he

meant it.

"We're okay. You don't think I'm a Nazi, huh?"

"What horseshit! Are you going to sue them?"

"Already have."

"It's crazy, Roger. How is your business?"

"Evaporated. That's why we need to talk. Car lease payments are going to be tough for a company with no revenue."

"That will not be a problem."

"Can you give me a ballpark idea of how much cash it will take for a buy-out?"

My current company car had about fourteen thousand dollars in remaining lease obligation. In commercial real estate leases it was common for a lessee to have to pay at least half of the remaining costs in cash to get out of a deal if it were possible to get out at all. Seven thousand dollars was going to be painful, but it was better than not dealing with the problem.

"Get it washed, bring me the keys and forget about it."

He was a Jew who read the same article that turned all the Gentiles against me. He had a rock solid contract and could have held my feet to the fire for the full fourteen thousand plus his legal fees incurred to get it if necessary. It was an act of incredible kindness, and my voice was breaking as we ended our call.

"I'll be over in an hour."

"I'll buy you lunch."

* * * * *

River Oaks Chrysler Plymouth sits at the intersection of Interstate 59 and Kirby Drive in Houston, one of the highest traffic locations in the country. Owned by Jack Helfman the dealership has become one of the highest volume outlets in the United States. With all the volume they still managed to greet regular customers by first name, and it was common to see Jack or his son Alan running back to the service department to check out a complaint. Bob had told me in the past that Jack had no debt of any kind in the business. The massive inventory along with several acres of the most desirable land in America easily made him one of the wealthiest men in Houston, but I often saw Jack as he had season tickets close to my regular seats for both the Houston Astros and the Houston Rockets -- in the blue collar sections.

Bob closed the door of his spartan office and looked me up and down.

"You look terrible."

"Good to see you too, Bob."

"What in the world happened to get them to do that story?"

For the fiftieth time I replayed all my experience with Doug Wyatt, culminating in my surprise deposition in *Wyatt v. Sakowitz*.

When I got to the part about Cobra, Bob turned pale. He just stared at me for a long time while seemingly searching for something he wanted to say very badly but could not.

"Roger, I'm going to tell you something that only two other people in the world know. I went to prison for Cobra."

He might as well have told me that George Bush was dumping Dan Quayle in favor of David Duke for the 1992 campaign. Cobra was one of the closest confidantes of long-term Houston mayor Kathy Whitmire, a nationally powerful member of the Democratic party, and regarded by many as the most feared man in Texas.

Bob had told us long ago of his transformation from a wealthy retired real estate developer to ex-con thanks to cocaine. He had served three years for some drug related charge, lost his family and wealth as a result, and been completely down and out when Jack Helfman took a chance on him to work in the leasing department. Many years after release Bob was the number one profit center for River Oaks, clean, and honest. We had never raised the details of his incarceration when seeing Bob and Susan socially, figuring that it was best left in the past. Whatever the past might have been he was a great guy now.

"Cobra and you..."

"The DEA wanted him. I had a coke problem, and was hanging out with lots of high rollers, staying up all night and running around in limousines. But when they finally busted me what they really wanted was what I knew about Cobra. When I refused to cooperate they gave me three years for misprision of a felony."

For the next hour Bob shared names and other details of

what is now an active Department of Justice investigation. Without sharing information potentially detrimental to pursuit of those involved Bob had referred two major cocaine traffickers to Cobra for assistance in obtaining legal representation. Cobra had evidently assisted many other criminals. He also had a public history of taunting the DEA and FBI for being incompetent, which went a long way to explain the strained relationship. Bob had personally been in Cobra's office when a client dumped a grocery sack with $450,000 in cash into Cobra's desk drawer as he held it open. The money was all from the sale of cocaine, and Cobra knew it.

All hell broke loose when the dealers did not get the complete release of charges as they expected. They came to Houston from Colombia specifically to kill Cobra. Bob had headed them off at the airport and convinced them to let it go, in effect saving Cobra's life. When the DEA looked into Bob Goldstein's role they had enough to charge him but made it clear that a deal was available if he would help nail Cobra. In great part relying on Cobra's advice Bob failed to do so, and wound up in prison.

"When I got out, Roger, I literally had no where to go, and not enough money for a sandwich. I called Cobra, and he told me it would be a 'conflict of interest' and 'too dangerous' for him to meet with me -- after I had just given him three years of my life. After that he wouldn't even return my phone calls. It was just last year that he did us the great favor of allowing Susan to insure his Jaguar. The son of a bitch is pure evil, and he set you up and sacrificed you."

I was convinced that everything Bob told me was true. When I got home from River Oaks the phone was ringing. It was Cobra.

"Roger, Judge Gregory is refusing to subpoena Doug Wyatt's life reading from Eternal Values, and I need to get you to go to the attorney's office and sign a sworn statement verifying your belief that the information is critical and that Doug will alter the tape if we don't get it now."

"Tell you what, Cobra, I'll fax a letter to you first thing in the morning."

"I need it now."

"I've got to go, Cobra."

In what would prove to be one of the most important steps in this long story I sent the following letter to Cobra via telefax on Saturday, September 21, 1991.

*****

September 21, 1991

Cobra
Address
Address

Personal and Confidential
Telefacsimile to Waiting Addressee

Dear Cobra:

For some time, I have made every conceivable effort to

cooperate with you in the understanding of the involvement in Douglas Wyatt in the Eternal Values cult. Unfortunately, during the recent past, information has come to my attention regarding your alleged involvement in activities which cause me great personal concern. Regardless of their truth or falsity, the various revelations come at a time when I have very real and valid concerns for the safety and well-being of the only thing I have left -- my family. As you can imagine, there is no interest on my part of any exploration or allegations about anyone at this point, especially you.

Until we have made our quiet exit from Houston, Texas, and the Wyatt v. Sakowitz debacle is behind me, I think it appropriate that any further communication be through my legal counsel.

Thank you for your understanding, and good luck.

Sincerely,

Roger D. Hall

* * * * *

There was total silence from Cobra after the transmission. He did not dispute the obvious allegation of serious misbehavior. He simply did not reply at all. I would not hear from him again until he was unexpectedly deposed by the *Chronicle's* attorneys a year later.

The amazing response to my transmission came from Coachwhip and Cottonmouth. From the start I thought it was completely relevant that the article had been run as a favor for a guy who associated with cocaine traffickers and laundered large amounts of drug money for them. If you were known by the company you keep, a jury was going to have some serious doubts about the management of the *Houston Chronicle*. Cottonmouth fought the entry of the information and deposition of Bob Goldstein every time I brought it up. My logic was typically that not only was it relevant it was ugly. Cobra had used homosexuality, drug abuse, and cult involvement on Doug Wyatt in the civil suit underlying all the problems. Why was using ugly information on him not fair play?

Cottonmouth ran through a series of arguments that included Goldstein's status as a convicted felon, his prior history of refusing to testify against Cobra, and the simple reality that involving Cobra in a conspiracy theory would open the door for "a smart guy to tell lots of creative lies instead of forcing the 'idiots' at the newspaper to think up their own lies."

I was still intent upon making the knowledge an issue until Cottonmouth finally told me that he thought we could do well without using the criminal behavior of Cobra as a weapon, and that doing so could very well make us the target of international cocaine traffickers who would not want Cobra and Goldstein throwing their names and work habits around in depositions available to the public. He finally had a legitimate point, and I agreed to let it go for the time.

Ultimately I would come to understand the real motivations of Cottonmouth in denying my repeated requests. -- and the power a criminal can wield at the highest levels of American government.

Early Hope

"God is usually on the side of big squadrons against little ones."

Roger De Bussy-Rabutin

At every opportunity Cottonmouth told me how slim the chances were of any plaintiff ever prevailing in a suit for libel.

By the end of January 1992 we had lined up over thirty witnesses to deny my having ever expressed adherence to any of the tenets of Eternal Values contributing to my demise. In my mind, the two most important of these were two former members of the cult who had been active in the central headquarters in New York City throughout the period of my recruitment by Doug Wyatt. Not only would they testify that I had broken from the process upon learning of the cult's true nature, one was going to say that she knew everything about everyone in the organization as part of her functioning as chief financial officer, but had no clue as to who I was.

One of the interesting sidelights of research was learning how deeply involved Douglas' socialite mother, Lynn Sakowitz

Wyatt had been in the activities of the cult. In her deposition for the *Wyatt v. Sakowitz* suit she had claimed to have no knowledge of anyone named Frederick von Mierers. We had already discovered one eyewitness to her travels to New York for herb therapy, as well as a local residential real estate broker from a famous Houston family who claimed that her mother had travelled with Mrs. Wyatt to Nantucket for lunch with Frederick.

We were looking forward to calling her to trial and asking if she considered herself to be a woman-hating, drug abusing neo-Nazi. It was obvious that she had been just one more unwitting target of Frederick and her own son, but she had actually taken many more steps than me in the path to membership in Eternal Values.

I was especially anxious to ask her if the insured gemstones that had unfortunately been stolen from her recently in New York were the ones that Douglas had sold to her on behalf of Frederick. If so, did she have them insured at the real value or the value established by Eternal Values commissioned appraisers? If the latter, I would then facetiously have Cottonmouth ask if we could have the phone number of the thief so that he and State Farm could help me out.

I had no vendetta against Lynn Wyatt, but the Wyatt family had quickly circled the wagons around Douglas rather than just admit his manipulation of friends and family for his guru. If Mrs. Wyatt refused to offer the truth to help me then the information we were accumulating seemed fair game in establishing that a pillar of the Jewish community could have known more than myself about the cult without ever having been a "member."

My first deposition went pretty much as expected. The complicating factor was that I had just had a vasectomy a few days before in response to my wife's rising blood pressure -- a condition which we attributed at least in part to too many years on birth control pills. Instead of a thirty minute out the door procedure performed by the head of the Department of Urology like I expected the surgery was done by a resident while the professor lectured. It took almost two hours and the anesthetic wore off about an hour into the process. I had literally chewed on a wet towel offered by a nurse who, unlike everyone else in attendance, had noticed the pain on my face.

I kept wanting to emphasize my deposition in Wyatt v. Sakowitz, especially some key responses to questions like "Were you a member of the cult?" My response had been one word -- no. If they based the article on the deposition, how did that square with the "former member" allegation in their cutline below my photo?

Hearst lead counsel, Hog-nose, steered the questions away from anything that I felt was relevant and focused on minute details of dates and times of meetings with Eternal Values members.

I also wanted to highlight the transcribed tape of my

interview with the author, Catherine Chriss, and multiple entries where she had reduced to writing that I had never been a member. They blew it off altogether.

They seemed to really thrive on the things that I had hoped to minimize, i.e., the life of real Eternal Values members behind the doors of their Manhattan apartments as described to us by our witnesses. Guys sitting on dildoes in full view of the other members to "rid themselves of ego," getting dressed up in ball gowns to be publicly sodomized by well-endowed male prostitutes, and group trips on psychedelic drugs were of infinitely more interest to the other side than they were to me. All I wanted to do was stay on the issue of whether I was a member or not. It played no role in the day's activities.

Unquestionably the most interesting portion of the day came when Catherine Chriss and one of the lesser attorneys left the room for an hour to read some materials we had delivered to them at the start of the deposition. One piece was the original version of the first chapter of this book. I was extremely uncomfortable physically that day and had left several times to change bandages. Catherine and the lawyer were coming back from another conference room as I was returning from one of my trips to the rest room. Catherine had obviously been crying. It was no doubt a stupid attitude for a plaintiff -- but I really felt sorry for her. She had always seemed a nice woman, and I surmised from her devastated look that the resistance to my suit was from the bean counters and lawyers. Several times during the afternoon she appeared to look at me with a "What have I done?" look on her face. It could have been my imagination, but I thought she was going to tell the truth in her deposition the next day. Cottonmouth summarily chastised me on the way home that night for ever thinking anything so stupid.

*****

I was in severe pain the next day and in no condition to go to Catherine's deposition. When Cottonmouth called me in the afternoon he was absolutely ecstatic.

"I just can't believe some of the things she said under oath."

"She seemed like an honest woman to me, Cottonmouth."

"Being honest has nothing to do with it. She should have been under strict orders from the *Chronicle* management to stick with the company line."

I knew that the rich, or at least Doug and his mother had little or no fear of perjury. I was terrified of it.

"Maybe she was scared of perjury."

"Roger, an old friend once told me that if there were no perjury there would be no need for the courthouse."

"What a great endorsement for the legal system, Cottonmouth. So do we have them by the ass now?"

"Not at all. We only have the facts and the jury. They

still have the law on their side."

* * * * *

They had a transcription of her deposition for me a few days later. If nothing else ever came of the whole war, I would be able to show her sworn statement to my children someday as the ultimate defense of my character. Suddenly it was all worthwhile.

From start to finish she had generally told the story the way it was with a few turns thrown in by Hog-nose to allow them, I would come to understand later, avoidance of totally discrediting the lies told by their subsequent witnesses.

To her credit Catherine Chriss gave the following responses to questions from my attorney Cottonmouth under oath:

The Extent of My Involvement in the Cult[1]

Cottonmouth: Ms. Chriss, would it be fair to say that your evidence of Roger Hall's involvement in Eternal Values based on your interview with him consist basically of the fact that he listened to tapes espousing the philosophy; read books that were provided to him by Eternal Values; discussed Eternal Values with Douglas Wyatt for some time; visited

---

[1] The Oral Deposition of Catherine Chriss, Case No. 91-052238 - Roger D. Hall vs. The Hearst Corporation and Catherine Chriss in the District Court of Harris County, Texas 152nd Judicial District, May 19, 1991, pp. 99-100.

	Frederick von Mierers twice in New York and purchased and wore gems that were prescribed to him by Eternal Values? Is that basically the behavior, the activity that you rely on as evidence of his involvement in the cult?
Chriss:	I think so. It's -- all of the material we went over in those things you mentioned.
Cottonmouth:	Okay. You never understood him to have been adherent or a believer in any doctrine that could be described as neo-Nazi, did you?
Chriss:	No, I did not.
Cottonmouth:	And you never understood him to have used as part of his involvement in Eternal Values used psychedelic or illegal drugs?
Chriss:	No, I did not.

<u>My Adherence to Eternal Values Dogma or Participation in Rites</u>[2]

Cottonmouth:	You also did not understand from Roger Hall or any other source that Roger Hall had been adherent of or a believer in doctrines that could be described as anti-Semitic, did you?
Chriss:	No, I don't think he was a believer in it; but there were times when he was aware that that's what the cult believed in.
Cottonmouth:	And he told you, did he not, that that was one of the reasons that he severed whatever connection he had with the cult?

---

[2] Ibid., pp. 101-103.

Chriss: Right.

Cottonmouth: And you didn't have any other information from any other source that would indicate that was untrue, did you?

Chriss: Right.

Cottonmouth: You also did not have any reason to believe that Roger Hall was anti-woman, either, in the sense of being expressly homosexual or hating women in some way?

Chriss: Right.

Cottonmouth: And you understood, did you not, that there were people in the cult who, in fact, it was claimed, did, in fact, hold anti-Semitic neo-Nazi beliefs?

Chriss: Correct.

Cottonmouth: And you also understood that there were people in the cult who did, in fact, engage in illegal drug use?

Chriss: Right, right.

Cottonmouth: You also understood that Roger Hall and other people said that there were homosexual and other sorts of unusual sex practices that were engaged in by people in the cult?

Chriss: Right.

Cottonmouth: You have been practicing journalism for how many years now?

Chriss: 12.

Cottonmouth: And you would agree with me that there are lots of different reasons why --

Chriss: Wait. I'm sorry, that should be nine.

Cottonmouth: All right. We're not a math major anyway, right?

Chriss: Yeah.

Cottonmouth: Okay. You would agree with me, would you not, that there are lots of different reasons why people agree to be interviewed by newspaper reporters?

Chriss: True.

Cottonmouth: What was your impression of Roger Hall's reason for wanting to be interviewed by a reporter or agreeing to be interviewed by a newspaper reporter?

Chriss: That he wanted to get the word out that -- what the cult was and he wanted to help end it or wreck it, stop it.

Her Attitude About Damage to Me[3]

Cottonmouth: But you said that being associated with Eternal Values in a newspaper article, in the largest newspaper in the state, was not going to help Mr. Hall's standing in the community?

---

[3]Ibid., p. 111

Chriss: I wasn't looking at how it was going to affect him. That doesn't really, you know, it's not here or there. I don't -- I'm looking at what the story's going to say and what it's going to tell people, not how it's going to affect him.

<u>Motivation for Rushing the Story to the Front Page of a Holiday Sunday Edition in Light of the Fact that the *Chronicle's* Largest Competitor *The Houston Post* Did Not Run the Story At All.</u>[4]

Cottonmouth: Do you have any disagreement with the assertion that this story was promoted to a large degree by Cobra?

Chriss: I'd say it was promoted by Cobra. I don't know that he promoted it to a large degree.

Cottonmouth: He was the one who originally talked to the *Chronicle* people about running it and he certainly cooperated when you were putting it together.

Chriss: I'd say that.

* * * * *

My favorite sports commentator had long been Don Meredith, former quarterback of the Dallas Cowboys. "Dandy" Don had made his mark in television during a Monday night game in the Houston Astrodome during one of the many losing seasons suffered by Oiler fans. It was late in the game, the Oilers

---

[4] Ibid., pp. 111-112.

were trailing by a huge margin, and some genius decided to scan the dome for a look at the few hundred fans left in the 50,000 seat facility. As they focused in on one pot bellied Texan with a head absolutely full of the dome's famous Big Beers, he raised his middle finger in a salute to Howard Cossell, ABC sports, and the entire American viewing public. In response to what could have been a miserably embarrassing moment for the network Meredith immediately spouted:

"Now there's a fan who thinks his team is number one!"

The response had everyone watching the game that night rolling in the floor with laughter, and converted a negative event into one of the great sports broadcasting moments of all time. Later in the telecast Meredith suddenly began to sing what was to become his trademark song for any team who was hopelessly behind and just killing time until the final whistle:

"Turn out the lights, the party's over. . ."

After reading Catherine Chriss' deposition for the third time I began to sing Don's song for the *Chronicle*. I just assumed that Cottonmouth was doing what I had always done when a client was clearly in control of a deal -- barraged them with negative information just to keep their expectations from becoming completely unreasonable. There was no way that the management of the *Chronicle* could foresee anything except a world class butt-kicking after their own reporter openly admitted that the damaging information was wrong in every single regard.

As icing on the cake we had gotten Susan Bearden (Doug's escort assigned by cult leader Frederick von Mierers) to allow us to audiotape eight hours of interviews with her. She detailed cult behavior, Douglas' worried comments about my resistance to recruitment, and a host of other issues in our favor from an eyewitness perspective.

We even gave copies of the tapes to our friends (and I assumed soon to be my employees) at the *Chronicle*.

It was looking like a landslide to me, but Shelly was close to making a decision on jobs. We were going to have to leave Houston if the suit did not end soon. Shortly after the deposition of Catherine Chriss' boss, Kyle Pope, it was time for the attorneys to set a trial date with the court. Cottonmouth called me after the attorneys for Hearst copied him on their notice, and this time he was beyond ecstatic. He was triumphant.

"The *Chronicle* requested mediation!"

I did not understand the importance of the event at all.

"So what?"

"A big newspaper would rather burn itself down than ever agree to anything less than total victory in a libel suit. They will never show weakness of any kind. Period. But they checked a box on the application for trial saying that they felt the case was appropriate for mediation. I had indicated that it was not appropriate for mediation because doing so would have looked like we were begging."

The significance of the event was becoming clear.

"So how long do I have to wait before they agree to get this thing behind them. We're out of cash, and going to have to move so Shelly can support us."

"Roger, it could still take years to get this done."

"What about my right to a speedy trial?"

"You don't have any right to a speedy trial in a civil action."

"So a crack dealer shoots a girl in the face at the intersection of Rice and Beechnut because his car is out of gas and he gets a speedy trial. And I am at the total mercy of opposing lawyers who are getting paid by the hour?"

"That's right."

"Is there anything about libel law that is not in their favor?"

"You're finally beginning to catch on, Roger."

We talked for a long time. Once again it became clear that what seemed to be such an obvious victory was still only one step in a long journey.

It was time to leave.

Leaving Home

"To withdraw is not to run away, and to stay is no wise action, when there's more reason to fear than to hope."

Cervantes, Don Quixote

My father once told me that you are lucky to have five real friends when you die. My father was an optimistic man.

By far the most insightful experience of all was learning firsthand the shallow nature of most human relationships. I had expected from the start that the commercial real estate brokerage community would go into a feeding frenzy of character assassination. They did nothing to disappoint me.

Commercial real estate is one of the last bastions of free enterprise with unlimited income and no entrance requirements, which unfortunately sets the stage for some pretty shallow people to get rich. For example, the most successful office leasing broker in Houston openly admits that his seven figure income is entirely the product of "baffling them with bullshit." That is, he and his counterparts make a slick presentation to corporate executives with little or no knowledge of office leasing. Their objective was to leave the recipient of the presentation confused and fearful, therefore dependent on the presenter for protection. The technique often worked, and the broker in question came to epitomize the credo of "success begets success," for he soon had such an overwhelming list of prior clients that his list sold his services. By 1991 he had a 10,000 square foot house in the exclusive Memorial area, complete with an indoor basketball court, several Mercedes, lots of Rolex watches, and a living area that Scorpion had once mystically described as done in "Ralph Lauren from one side to the other." The only mystifying thing to me was that this guy had never set foot on a college campus. No kidding. He had never taken even the most elementary courses in math, statistics, accounting, finance, or anything else -- yet he lighted the way on hundreds of extremely complex multimillion dollar decisions. There is no justification for educational elitism, and of all people I firmly believe that many of our greatest leaders and citizens have been people like my father who simply did not have the opportunity for formal education. But my father had never tried to direct a major oil company in its placement of $50 million of shareholder wealth in a real estate transaction. Armed with this little known reality of the business, it is probably not much of a surprise that commercial brokerage attracted a large number of former computer, copier, and insurance salesmen. It was certainly not a surprise to me that from the beginning I had been an outcast in the brokerage community by virtue of my analytical rather than social approach. The animosity grew as my success grew, and many of my competitors were dumbfounded that someone who combed his hair and shined his shoes so infrequently could ever succeed in such an image-driven line of work.

The point is that it was neither surprising nor especially painful when every day brought another anecdote of a sales meeting or broker conversation where the topic was along the lines of "whether Dougie was the pitcher or the catcher in our homosexual affair." They were, by and large, small-minded, mean people, and to engage in small-minded, mean things was simply a logical expression of their nature.

My mounting psychological problems were definitely magnified as the result of a lack of support from those whom I had expected to be of deeper character. A particularly tough experience came one evening at the Rice Foods market near our home where we did most of our grocery shopping. Rounding a corner near the register I came face to face with a marketing executive from Coca-Cola Foods. We had worked together for more than ten years. I had trained him in the art of corporate (and self) defense on their multiple sales office leases around the country, and we had worked together to implement a standardization program that won him great praise internally and played a significant role in his promotion. When he moved on I stayed behind to train three more of his subordinates in exactly the same manner over an eight year period. He and I had remained friends, our wives had become friends, and we had even played a role in their move from the distant suburbs to our neighborhood. The day they moved in we were there with wine and greetings. But when they saw me coming around the corner that day in the supermarket, they looked straight into my eyes, halted, and walked out of the store, leaving their partially filled basket behind without uttering a word. As luck would have it my daughter's elementary school play was that same evening. As we entered the auditorium I saw the wife of a guy I had helped to save at the Horne Company by literally giving him some transactions to work on from my client base during a period when he was struggling. We had been to countless parties and other social functions together. When I said hello from a distance of around three feet she stared at me as if I had just descended from the ramp of one of Frederick von Mierers' spaceships. She said nothing as she got up and moved to the back of the seating area.

The stories are countless, and dredging them up for this chapter is proving to be a more difficult experience than I had expected so I'll let it end with the understanding that people place an incredible level of importance on what they read in the paper. From my personal experience they often place more importance on the written word of strangers than on years of their own observations.

Maybe a group wielding this kind of power over the

minds of Americans should be held to a high standard of credibility rather than no standard at all. But I'll save that for Chapter Twelve.

* * * * *

With all due respect for my father's theory, I was not completely abandoned. Two people stand out immediately in my mind as individuals who totally disregarded the flood of misinformation in favor of our friendship. Matt Miller, the former Coca-Cola executive who had moved to the spun-off Maryland Club Foods group proved himself to be a stellar example of practicing Christianity. He is one of four completely and totally honest people I have ever known in business. That is not to say that there are not others who are basically honest, but most businessmen will submit to bending their morals a bit under extreme pressure. Matt stood up to every challenge, including one coming from an unethical and dishonest tyrant who was the only president of Coca-Cola Foods ever to be fired, without once in the twelve years we worked together even considering any action that was not completely honest and fair. From the day the article appeared until today Matt has backed me up.

Another great source of support was Bob Dey. I had met Bob when he became interested in my Drug Free Business Initiative (DFBI) as part of his job as Demand Reduction Agent for the DEA in Houston. To a great extent Bob is individually responsible for that program having become the national success it is today, even though there have been plenty of others who came along to take the credit long after he and I beat the streets of Houston trying to turn up enough interest to have a business leader breakfast. When the Board of Directors of DFBI (all of whom had been selected and recruited by me) chose to disregard personal experience in favor of a tabloid article, the administrator of the program, Calvina Fay, had called me to discuss stepping down due to the board's concern about negative publicity. It was like having your first-born child stab you in the stomach with an ice pick. Bob was the one member of the program who never wavered in his support and belief. I had known lots of government types who spent half their day deciding what to have for lunch and the other half figuring out how to cover their ass. Unlike others in DEA who will appear in later chapters Bob was not afraid to believe in what he knew to be the truth when jumping on the "Dump Roger" bandwagon would have been much easier. He is the kind of friend few people are fortunate enough to have, and as long as Bob and Janet Reno are in the Department of Justice there will be at least two honest people in law enforcement.

Even though Bob and Matt have proven themselves to be two of the five friends my dad had talked about neither of them had any commercial real estate deals for me to work on. Between clinical depression, assassination by competitors, and abandonment by former clients it was getting to the point where I knew we were going to run out of money. Our rule, once we adjusted to my high income, was to always keep enough after tax cash on hand to cover two years of our total debt in the event of an emergency. By the time it was clear that Shelly was going to have to abandon her commitment to academic medicine and get a job we were down to sixteen months. Any move was going to be expensive, and I desperately needed to generate some kind of income no matter how bad I felt.

Ten years before the article appeared I had made a public service call on a small company known as the Owen Company. They managed hospital pharmacies around the country, were growing rapidly, and were eager to learn what I had to say about alleviating Houston's overwhelming traffic congestion problems through a program known as the Regional Mobility Plan. Their director of administration was a charming lady who went by her nickname -- Andy. Andy Marlatt had been one of the original members of the company, which by 1981 had grown to around 200 employees and by 1991 was widely recognized as one of the best run and fastest-growing private companies in America.

Andy had become one of my closest friends as the years went by, as had her boss Carl Isgren. In what must be a great source of comfort to shareholders Carl was one of those presidents who was clearly deserving of the epithet used on George Halas: "George throws nickels around like man-hole covers." I had invited Carl to join the central support group for

Congressman Jack Fields of Texas' eighth congressional district. As the months of association rolled into years Carl and Andy became bigger and bigger forces in my business life from both economic and ethical standpoints. As the company grew they remained loyal to me, and what had once been a small account had become one of the largest in Houston.

Carl had become interested in my public service activities. He had a history of board level participation in a great program known as the Living Bank organ donor registry. If it were possible to be honest to a fault, Carl Isgren was honest to a fault -- and so conservative that it was unthinkable that he could ever have an open mind about something like Doug Wyatt and Eternal Values. I just assumed that Owen, now known as Owen Healthcare, Inc. would disappear in the mist like all my other clients.

I would learn much later that on the Tuesday after Labor Day 1991 Andy's desk had been covered with copies of the article brought in by other managers wanting to know why they were doing business with someone like me. She not only stood by me but insisted that Carl call me in for a closed door discussion. We had it, and they kept me on to handle their real estate transactions for the entire period of transition to a new home and life. If it had not been for the loyalty and support of Carl and Andy the process would have been much, much worse. Maybe it would have been unbearable.

One of the many positive influences Carl had on my life

was getting me to train for and run a marathon. After months of arduous training I got a severe case of the flu two weeks before the 1990 Houston Tenneco Marathon. I was barely out of bed and extremely dehydrated the day of the race. The first fifteen miles were okay, but my legs began to lock up around mile seventeen and I began to have thoughts of trying again the next year. Mile nineteen is notorious for being the worst for long distance runners, especially new ones. It is then that your body has depleted its readily accessible energy stores and you hit what is known as the "wall." It was looking bleak.

Arriving at the mile nineteen marker and water stand it was clear that there was no way for me to finish the remaining seven miles. Looking to the right for a place to lie down I saw Carl. He had come to cheer me on, perhaps realizing that the whole silly idea was his in the first place. A strange thing happened. It was just not possible to let him down. He was the kind of leader that you could not bring yourself to disappoint. We waived, smiled, and I headed on toward downtown Houston. During the twenty-third mile my legs locked so hard that my knees would not bend and I had to finish the last three and a half miles in a straight legged fast shuffle. My goal had been three hours and thirty minutes, roughly eight-minute miles. It took an extra twenty-six minutes but I got in under four hours, collapsing briefly just after the finish line.

Carl and Andy taught me about the depth of loyalty still available in the best of America's businesses. Carl taught me about the limits of human endurance. If it had not been for their lessons and support this fight would never have been finished.

* * * * *

Regardless of the support offered by Owen there was no way I could run a business having only one client with sporadic needs. The brokerage community was taking every opportunity to share the *Chronicle* story with potential clients and my condition was not conducive to fighting through the resistance. I had no way of knowing when, if ever, it would be. Some dramatic steps had to be taken, and taken quickly.

Shelly had been the target of initial humiliation from some small-minded members of the residency program, and I wondered what would happen if she tried to seek positions in established practices outside Houston. Would the faculty of the University of Texas system refuse to give her recommendations because of me?

The faculty proved themselves to be the kind of people I had always assumed them to be. She got the excellent letters of recommendation she deserved, which was particularly heartening in light of the fact that she had to relinquish the position of head resident, thereby leaving them in the lurch on management for the coming year.

Since there are not a lot of M.D., Ph.D. females who

graduate first in their medical school class and then choose to go into the worst paying area of medicine, pediatrics, it was not surprising that recruiters and practices in need of assistance jumped all over her applications. She was inundated by calls from all over the country.

For the first time in memory I actually stayed out of her way as she went through a systematic process that eventually reduced her options to positions in Missouri, Arizona, and Florida. The Missouri position was a hospital-sponsored underwriting of a private practice. In essence, they get you started so you can send them business later. The idea of returning to Joplin, Missouri, the city of our youth was the sharpest dual-edged sword I had ever seen. Shelly would return as the woman who clearly escaped the Midwest chains of role assignment for little girls. She would be one of the gods in a town where doctors are still treated as something beyond mortal. We would be close to our parents, providing them easy access to their grandchildren for the first time. She would make the most money available to her on a guaranteed basis but once again be in the position of working eighty hours per week or more. In the end, wanting to see her children grow up overrode her desire to have her parents do it instead.

The Arizona position was hands down my favorite. They were serious enough contenders that we did not feel dishonest about accepting their offer for a tour of the Prescott area. We had taken the kids to the Grand Canyon once, but I was in the middle of a major transaction and remember spending most of my time looking for pay phones. As we headed north out of Phoenix on Interstate 17 the sun was just beginning to set. When we hit the first area with an unobstructed mountain view the distant peaks were bathed in thousands of different red and yellow hues. I have very little visual ability or appreciation, but that evening provided the most beautiful landscape I'd ever seen.

The next day proved Prescott to have as much charm as it did beauty. The prices of houses proved reasonable. The pediatric practice, like so many others in the country, was completely overrun by business. They had closed the practice, meaning that no new patients were being taken, many months before our arrival. It was an incredible financial opportunity.

Shelly spent he day with a female pediatrician who was the newest member of the practice. We were to have dinner with the two primary partners in the evening. I spent the day with the husband of the pediatrician, who was a realtor in the area. We had literally been in his truck less than ten minutes when he began telling me about the politics, infidelity, spouse abuse, extortion, and humiliation rampant in the group. Shelly heard the same thing.

By dinner that night we knew that Cinderella did not have a wart on her nose. She had a malignant tumor the size of a basketball. Ever the optimist, Shelly was convinced that she could distance herself from the problems. Unknown to her at the time, one of her fellow residents had taken me aside at a recent party and told me that Shelly was having an affair with a good-looking young resident from Louisiana. They had arranged their call schedules so that they could spend their nights at Hermann Hospital together, usually on the same service or on a service close to each other. The bearer of the news went on to tell me that Shelly had confided to a few friends that she was unsure of my involvement in Eternal Values and planned to leave me immediately upon completion of her residency to marry this fellow resident.

The woman telling the story proved to be little more than a psychotic trouble-maker. She had a crush on the man she accused my wife of spending nights with behind the locked doors of the resident sleep rooms, but he had no interest in her. The entire story was a fabrication, and God only knows why she needed to do that to me at the time. But depression has a way of making fabrications real, and vice versa. I had spent many nights the month before the Prescott trip looking at the ceiling and imagining a custody hearing where a vicious lawyer hired by my wife would be reading the *Chronicle* story to a judge to whom his firm had just made a big campaign contribution. I was not strong enough at the moment to handle her jumping into a medical business where the ego of the managing partner somehow allowed him to justify public knowledge of his regularly pounding the receptionist on a stirrup-equipped examining table between the hours of six, when everyone else went home, and eight, when he quit handling "after-hours call" for the group.

At dinner that night I focused my conversation on the wife of the culprit. She put him through medical school and bore and raised his children, only to endure his openly spending as many nights as he chose away from her and the kids at the home of the receptionist. She was a wonderful woman. He was an asshole. Prescott came to be a magnificent opportunity despoiled by the male ego.

What had seemed to me to be the incredibly distant third of the finalists Shelly had chosen had secretly always been her first choice. From the time the Nemours Foundation came through town during her second year of residency pitching healthcare for poor children in areas with little or no pediatric service she knew that she someday wanted to make a difference with her life. There was a lot more money to be made looking in the ears of, and writing Ritalin prescriptions for, the neurotic children of affluent yuppies. But she had never cared much for money and cared even less after the events following Labor Day 1991 proved what a hollow victory financial success can be.

By July 1992 we were on our way to a place I could not have found on the United States map six months before.

* * * * *

Our final social engagement was the Friday night before we were to leave on Tuesday. We went to dinner with Bob and

Susan Goldstein. I'll never forget the way Bob helped me when the chips were down, or the support they both showed us in the darkest days.

The day the moving trucks came I went to say goodbye to Carl Isgren. I do not recall ever having heard of two powerful businessmen having their eyes filled with tears because one was moving. Carl kept my Drug Free Business Initiative, which was like one of my children, alive until it was strong enough to support itself. He is the greatest man I've ever known in business.

Mike and Andy Marlatt came over to see us and the moving trucks off. Andy will always be a treasured friend -- effectively the sister of a secluded only child. Mike loves her as much as any human can love another. They deserve each other.

Ken Harris cleaned our houses for almost ten years. As a gay man in Houston, cleaning toilets was perhaps the highest opportunity available. He proved to be one of our closest and best friends. I want to think that our support of him in the decision to enter residential real estate brokerage had something to do with one of the most incredible metamorphoses in business history. After less than two years he is his company's top producer and made more than $15,000 for himself in a recent month. Ken was crying as we closed the doors.

Laure Kocian came from Shiner, Texas to escape the small-town-girl syndrome. She ended up in our garage apartment while attending the University of Houston, effectively raising our babies for almost three years. She quickly stopped being hired help and became a permanent member of the family. We wanted her to go to Florida with us, but the economics were not there. And her family still had some doubts. She stayed behind.

In one of the most bizarre of all the events my best friend from high school had called after the article. Mitch Williams had called every R. Hall in the phone book because neither of us had any idea the other lived in Houston. We were able to meet the respective wives and children -- and have some great times together before leaving. The power of the media pulled us back together, and the power of the media ripped us apart again.

My last act in Houston, Texas was to answer the phone. Service was to be cut off at any time, and I was about to unplug the phone that had been given to me as an award for being the top producer at my first white collar job, when it rang. It was Dr. O'Donnell -- the psychiatrist who had helped so much but that I could no longer afford to see. We talked for about ten minutes or so, but the last few lines are the ones I remember.

"How are you holding up?"

"Look at my heroes, Doc. Keith and John always performed better under pressure."

"Tell me the truth."

"I don't have any clue what the truth is Doc, but I'm still moving."

"I just want it to be over for you."

"It'll be over when God wants it to be over."

* * * * *

Then we were gone.

November Rain

"Animals are not brethren, they are not underlings; they are other nations, caught with ourselves in the net of life and time."

Henry Beston, The Outermost House

"To die is different from what any one supposed, and luckier."

Walt Whitman, "Song of Myself," Leaves of Grass

In order to combat the rampant materialism of our Houston environs I had taken my daughter to the city pound on her seventh birthday and allowed her to decide if she wanted to save a kitten or get the high-tech roller blades she thought she wanted.

We took a scrawny, yellow alley kitten home, and she stuck with the old roller blades from Target. It was one of the best days my daughter and I ever had together.

My wife had been a cat person all her life, and for nearly eighteen years there had always been some assortment of strays from McDonald's parking lots or apartment complex dumpsters living with us. With the single exception of a Siamese named Pooh, I totally ignored them. They got a lot of attention, but all they got from me was can opener operation and litter box cleaning. I loved dogs but saw little or no value in cats. There was no animosity, just indifference. By all manner of reasonable observation they felt pretty much the same about me.

Elyssa's yellow cat came to be known as "Milo." He was named after one of the stars of "Milo and Otis" -- her favorite movie at the time.

In keeping with my established policy of cat avoidance I pretended to have no interest in Milo, but he was proving to be one of the smartest animals I had ever known. The other four cats, including an arguably intelligent McDonald's parking lot refugee known as Roo, knew very well that jumping on the desk in my home office was an offense that would be met immediately with fits of screaming and eraser throwing. Even if the glass doors were open they kept their distance.

Not Milo, though. He would come to the corner of the desk and peer around at me working on the computer. Over the course of several weeks he inched closer every day until he finally came in one day and jumped up in front of me as I was reading. Instead of moving around and becoming an annoyance he always moved to the front of the desk and promptly went sound asleep. Every day thereafter he did the same -- never wanting any attention, just hanging out.

As the trouble and depression mounted, Milo had been

subjected to literally hundreds of replays of the ballad "November Rain" by Guns N' Roses. November Rain was a very unusual song for the band and quite unlike anything else written by Axl Rose. It deals with depression, a topic that Axl (as a diagnosed manic depressive) seemed to know quite a lot about. It specifically deals with the loss of someone you love. I listened to November Rain over and over and over during the period after the unscrupulous female resident had told me that my wife was about to leave me. My experience with the song was published in a reader-submitted special called "Our Lives, Our Music" in the 25th anniversary issue of *Rolling Stone* magazine.

I had always been hyperactive. Sitting still for more than thirty minutes was simply beyond my ability. During these worst times I would sit at the desk for as much as six hours at a time without getting up. No food, no work, just the CD player locked on repeat with November Rain playing.

Milo began to inch closer to me day by day, and eventually came to pat my hands with his paws. It was impossible to ignore, and it even made me smile. We began to spend hours listening to the same song while playing our game of paw slapping. When he grew tired of the game he would crawl into my lap and go to sleep.

Milo and I had become friends.

* * * * *

The thousand-mile trip from Houston to Jacksonville quickly became the trip from Hell. Shelly's parents had wanted to help, and they were a great deal of assistance with the kids while we had been packing. But a thousand-mile car ride is tough on anyone, and Shelly's dad had a very bad heart problem. From the first entrance ramp I was scared to death he was going to have another heart attack.

After what only seemed like four or five years we reached the Florida line on I-10 and stopped at a La Quinta Inn outside Pensacola for the night. We were supposed to close on the new house in two days so the schedule was tight. We were up at five the next morning to get started. Elyssa was carrying Milo to the car in a plastic pet carrier, and in her early morning drowsiness tripped and dropped him. The door was loose, and Milo got half-way out through a gap in the top. Shelly quickly pinned him against the sidewalk with her bare hands. Milo had never been outside and was excitable by nature. He flipped out and ripped her arms up in panic, at one point biting her thumb so hard that he pierced the nail and his tooth went all the way through to the other side. In one of the most impressive displays of pain tolerance I have ever seen, she held on tight.

Shelly's mother was screaming at Elyssa, Elyssa and Jeremy were crying, Shelly was bleeding profusely, and I was fumbling in the half-light to get the damned cage back together. The door finally clicked, but when we tried to stuff him back inside the door popped out again and he took off at full speed.

I wanted to stay and look for him, and Shelly and I fought for half an hour about my giving her power of attorney to close on the house. But there was no way she could make the last four hundred miles alone.

So we looked everywhere in the complex again and left signs with the lady at the front desk. But it was hopeless.

Milo was gone.

* * * * *

Mayflower Transit had contractually agreed to have four people on hand to unload. They provided two. I ripped my back up trying to keep them from dropping the piano. It rained like crazy all day when we arrived.

The two movers we did have were nice, family-oriented Hispanic guys, and I ended up giving the driver an autographed photo of President Bush for his eight-year-old daughter in Mexico. It was her birthday and her daddy was fifteen hundred miles away. Shortly thereafter he dropped my Minolta copier and it bounced like a basketball. It took a year of fighting with Mayflower and the unenlightened bureaucrats of the Interstate Commerce Commission to get it repaired.

I spent my first night as a resident of Florida lying in a tub of hot water, eating Advil, and wondering how Milo was faring.

* * * * *

Things began to level out in a few days. We had great neighbors and their were lots of kids to play with, and the area was really beautiful -- essentially an island of development surrounded by protected wetlands.

Ten days after arrival I had a dream that if we went back Milo would be waiting at the hotel. We called the hotel at least twice every day, and he had reportedly been spotted around the dumpster by one of the maids.

If there was any doubt in my wife's mind about the total loss of my sanity it was removed when I announced to her the next morning that the kids and I were going to Pensacola for the day to get Milo. She told me it was a wild goose chase but had a hundred other things to worry about -- so we were off.

We combed the grounds at La Quinta, went to the pound, the humane society, and even door to door in the neighborhood around the hotel asking if anyone had seen Milo. It was beginning to get dark, Elyssa was beginning to cry, and I was beginning to wonder why we had come at all. It had only served to break my daughter's heart all over again.

I put my arm around her as we finished our last walk around the parking lot and dumpster of La Quinta. She called for him one last time, and from the other side of the parking lot we heard a faint meow. She called again, and he answered again.

We ran to a small house trailer. Milo was talking up a storm from underneath the trailer. I knocked on the door and the lady living there listened to the story, took one look at Elyssa, and told us to go ahead and try to rescue him. She had seen him on several occasions scratching around in a pile of cat litter a neighbor had dumped on the ground behind her trailer.

Milo was much too dignified to be digging latrines in ordinary dirt.

As my ongoing luck would have it the trailer was tightly encircled with aluminum skirting that had been honed to a surgical edge. The skirting was shielded by a tightly packed row of rose bushes. By the time I found a hole to look through, my arms were raw meat.

When I finally saw him it was clear that he was on his last leg. He had no clue about how to forage for food and was afraid of his own shadow anyway. My guess was that other cats and dogs had kept him from doing any good at the dumpster. He was literally a walking yellow skeleton and absolutely terrified. As I reached to pick him up he bolted out a hole in the other side and began running at full speed. I backed out, jumped over the roses, and gave chase. He darted around the brick house of the trailer park's owner and disappeared. Remembering that Milo was a smart guy, I thought that maybe he had gotten around the house a little too fast. Peering behind the hedge I found a small portal in the bricks that had lost its screen covering. Looking inside I spotted Milo forty feet away, trembling underneath a wooden support beam. He was not going anywhere near any human being, and there was no way to reach him or even get under the house.

In less than an hour we blocked the opening with a rock, made friends with the elderly couple in the house, checked into the La Quinta, left a message for mom, got a can of cat food and some heavy work gloves at Wal-Mart, and rented an animal trap from A to Z rental. There was no way I was leaving our cat to die of starvation in a strange and hostile place.

The kids went to sleep about ten. I checked the cat food in the end of the live trap every hour till two in the morning. At around two-thirty Milo sat just in front of the cage and refused to move. Even though fueled by anti-depressants I was exhausted. I finally just looked at him and said:

"Milo, I can't take any more. Let's go home."

He walked into the cage and the trap door failed to work. But the cat food was his favorite -- turkey and giblets with gravy. He didn't even notice when I tripped it by hand.

Shelly was amazed, Elyssa and Jeremy were ecstatic, and Milo was nearly dead. But school was out for the summer so he didn't touch the ground for several days except to have one of his ten scheduled feedings or to use the new extra large litter box. He slowly began to look like the old Milo.

The other cats had already decided to be lizard chasing, tree climbing "Country Cats," but Milo ran in the other direction any time a door to the outside was opened. He spent most of his days on the desk in my new basement office. He could tell that I was too busy to play -- trying to get ready for a new career as just another broker in someone else's company. And Milo was somehow too mature now for silly adolescent games anyway. He just wanted to be around.

A week into the new job I got up to get ready before the forty-mile drive into Jacksonville. Shelly was in the kitchen making a pot of coffee.

"Did you hear the ruckus at the pond last night?"

"I was dead the minute the pillow made contact."

"I almost got up. It sounded like a cat fight."

I walked down the winding path leading toward Black Creek to the pond used by the former owner for shiners and other game fish bait. On the creek side lay the stiff and partially eaten body of Milo. He had evidently gathered his courage and snuck by one of the kids for his first adventure in the wild. His killer could have been a hawk, an owl, wild dogs, or even a Florida panther.

I buried him where he died, along with a small pewter cross that had sat on my desk for years. Something dug his body up and chewed on it some more that night. I covered the grave with concrete blocks, and whatever did the digging the first night dug in from the side and carried his body down to the creek the next night. I picked up what was left, told him goodbye for the last time, and tossed his body in the dark water.

For the only time in all the events following September 1, 1991, I took my anger up with God. Looking at the sky above the creek I cried like a three year old and screamed.

"You didn't have to take my cat. There was no reason to take my Goddamned cat. He didn't do anything to you. It isn't fair. You had no right to take my cat."

*****

This book is full of strange stories, most of which are supported by sworn statements or otherwise verifiable records from sources other than myself. Other than the adoption record, there is no external support for the end of this story about Milo -- but it is true.

The night of my tirade against God I had another dream. Milo was in a wire cage, looking directly at me and speaking in a human voice:

"You'll find me in thirteen."

That was all he said.

The next morning I looked in the yellow pages to see if Clay County had a pound. They called it "Animal Control," and it was just a little out of the way on my daily trip into Jacksonville. The lady at the front desk told me she didn't remember any yellow cats, but I was welcome to look around. There was nothing in the cat area.

Leaving the adult animal area on my way out I passed some cages full of kittens. In one of the top cages there were three gray striped alley cats -- and one yellow adolescent. He looked like he had been through a garbage disposal and just sat in the back staring silently at me while his three cell mates wrestled for position at the front door.

I went to the reception area and told the lady which one I wanted. She pulled up his file and told he had been found in a Middleburg dumpster the night Milo died. She asked me if I noticed the cage number or his collar number. I had not.

She called back to the area for information while filling out the adoption form. I watched as she filled in the blanks.

Sex: Male.

Age: Approximately five months.

Color: Yellow.

Cage Number: Thirteen.

* * * * *

Elyssa wanted to name the new cat Milo after her old cat. He sometimes goes outside with the other cats in the daytime, but he is the only one that always insists on coming inside when it begins to get dark. He is also the only cat that can come into my office without getting bombed by an eraser.

The Day of Transition

"Fear is the main source of superstition, and one of the main sources of cruelty."

Bertrand Russell, <u>Unpopular Essays</u>

At last, it seemed, things would be getting better. Shelly was settling into her pediatric practice and giving me some comfort in my battered hope that all things eventually work out for the good. The pediatric clinic she ran for the Nemours Foundation in Green Cove Springs, Florida, had been the subject of a considerable amount of physician turnover prior to her arrival. Much as she had been doing with me for twenty years, she immediately instilled a sense of stability and confidence in her staff and patients.

My initial impression was that her patient population might be short on money, but the vast majority were sincere about trying to take good care of their children. They came in old cars, pushed used strollers, and sometimes dressed their children in clothing from rummage sales, but there was nothing wrong with their commitment to motherhood. I often thought about sending photos of a poor mother laughing with her babies to Doug Wyatt's international socialite mother, but not only was it much too late she would not have gotten the message anyway.

Early in Shelly's new job we got a feel for how the various physicians lured to remote areas of Florida really felt about the locals. Most were attracted by the stability of Alfred DuPont's money and the promise of a more relaxed lifestyle than their peers, but my guess was that over the long haul this kind of work also demanded a real compassion for the lower socioeconomic class patient population. Data to support my theory came early and unexpectedly in the form of a violent eruption in one of the first group physician meetings Shelly attended. When an administrator made the mistake of using the term "indigent" in referring to the overall population served by the Nemours satellite clinics, a middle-aged female pediatrician, who had clearly been a student radical in her younger days, jumped to her feet and screamed:

"Don't call them indigent!"

As every faced turned to her, she continued: "They don't have money. They may live in trailers. They may not play golf at Sawgrass Country Club, but they are damned sure not without intelligence and pride. I'd like to see how well some of you would do if you had to operate on what they raise their families on -- and they do a good job. Calling them indigent is insulting, and they know it is insulting."

To the best of my knowledge, that term was not used again by anyone. Hearing the story made me feel even more strongly that although we had been through a meat grinder, it had somehow resulted in our coming to a good place. Even though the pay was well below the national average, the foundation repeatedly succeeded in recruiting only the best of the medical school and practicing pediatric communities. To see this level of loyalty in people of such intellect was refreshing. It almost restored my faith in mankind. Almost.

Nothing is perfect, and life in northern Florida was no exception. From the beginning I was fascinated by the proliferation of close families and the widespread adherence to what I regarded as fundamentalist values. Women were still chattel to a great extent, as evidenced by the many fathers who continued to mistake my wife for a nurse in her clinic. That, however, was a mistake that would only be made once.

Football fanaticism reached levels unparalleled anywhere in the United States. Having grown up in the heart of the Big Eight, and then living in Texas with the maniacal followers of the Southwest Conference, there was little reason to believe college football could be taken any more seriously. But in the land of Gators, Seminoles, and Hurricanes, football followed only God and family in importance, and then only in the off season. During my first month at the new job in Jacksonville, our office manager's husband had been whirled around on his barstool at a local hangout after one of the games and punched hard enough in the eye to need twelve stitches. He had honestly thought that his comment regarding the parental fidelity of Florida State's offensive backfield was audible only to his University of Florida buddy, but that was not the case. Stories abounded of similar violence resulting from the popular local recipe of one part brain, two parts team spirit, and three parts alcohol.

The nation got a feel for the extent of area fervor when Jacksonville beat out St. Louis and Baltimore for the last of the pro football franchises awarded in 1993. Regarded as a one thousand to one long shot, not only did Jacksonville win but immediately rewarded the NFL's risk-taking by selling every available ticket for every game during the first three years less than a month after the announcement-- at the highest season ticket prices in league history.

Close families and football fanatics were just fine with me, especially since the chances were extremely remote that I would ever be accosted while rooting for the Rice Owls. On the other hand, it had quickly become clear that expressing a liberal position on any subject was an unnecessary and dangerous risk. Abortion, gay rights, AIDS funding, military cutbacks, and many other potentially explosive subjects were best left alone. While I continued to judge even the strangest of people on an individual basis, open-minded discussion about alternative lifestyle or any nontraditional belief was clearly taboo in this area known as "Baja Georgia" to those in the southern end of the state.

The extent of this intellectual rigidity became painfully clear during a private dinner at the home of one of my son's new friends. They are wonderful people, great parents, and had gone out of their way to make us feel at home in the area. But our evening alone with them proved to be deeply disturbing.

After the steaks, mushrooms, and desserts I was ready for some time on the couch. No longer driven by a desire for the incessant conversation created by alcohol before, during, and after meals I was merely a spectator to the all encompassing discourse between my wife and our host on a wide variety of issues. They agreed on almost everything until she made an unknowing step into an emotional mine field by stating that one of her close friends, and one of the best pediatric surgeons in the country, was a lesbian. The comment was made in an offhand way and certainly did not indicate that she personally had any interest in nontraditional sexual roles of any kind. But the short fuse had been lit. Leaning back in his chair, our friend's face immediately went beet red, and he began a verbal tirade that went on for several minutes.

"I thought you had your shit together in a little bitty ditty bag. I said to myself 'Now here is a woman that has it all together,' and you sit here in my dining room, eating my food, and tell me that you are the friend of a homosexual."

Neither of us had any idea this was going to happen, and our friend's wife was clearly becoming uneasy, but he was becoming more agitated by the second.

"Do you mean to tell me that you would let a homosexual cut on your children? Good God Almighty! When you know they all have AIDS? Hell, we don't know anything about that disease. You don't know any better than me if that stuff can be passed through gloves in surgery. God Almighty, and I thought I knew you."

I quietly sank into a dark depression as the ranting continued. . . slowly fading to a faint demonic soliloquy. Observing from a great distance, I was comfortable that Shelly was simply going to weather the storm rather than make matters even worse by mounting a counterattack. The rest of my evening was spent wondering how these same people would treat me if a copy of the *Chronicle* article ever made its way into the area. Assemblage of all relevant facts prior to arrival at a firm position did not seem to be the order of the day in Baja Georgia, and the chances were remote that anyone would read depositions of the defendants stating that I was none of the things the article implied before forming an opinion. Throughout my prior passage through the valley of the shadow of death, and after all the damage to what had once been my soul, I held firmly to the belief that no one had the right to hate all homosexuals any more than Hitler and Frederick von Mierers had the right to hate all Jews. It was suddenly clear that this belief would not be tolerated here, and certainly not if espoused by a former member of a new age, neo-Nazi cult that believed homosexual men were the highest form of human evolution. In our new home, as in the legal system, truth was secondary to rules of order.

It was far and away the worst night of our new life, and I wondered how long it would be possible to keep the devastating lies in my past. The answer to the question came faster and was more disturbing than I could have ever expected.

* * * * *

Like all business people, the owner of Atlantic Commercial Properties in Jacksonville, Robert Brathune, had an agenda of his own when making the decision to bring me into his organization. His young company was growing like wildfire, a growth that caused considerable distress among the area's older and more established commercial real estate brokerage firms. This success stood to reason since I had quickly formed the opinion that putting someone like Robert -- an honors graduate of the Naval Academy who could safely return F-4 fighter jets to the deck of an aircraft carrier on a stormy night -- into brokerage was akin to allowing Reggie Jackson to play in Little League.

One of the well known but seldom discussed tools of our high income profession was to never admit lack of expertise on any given transaction to any client. When they say "Can you do this?" your reply is always, "You bet," regardless of your actual level of experience with the type of transaction. Following a calm assertion of competence, you run like mad back to the office and hope that someone knows what the client was talking about. In the case of Robert's company, one of his agents had discovered that General Electric Capital Corporation was considering moving from their current office building at the end of their lease in early 1994. Commercial real estate brokers are paid a percentage of the gross cash flow generated by the new lease. In this case, the commission could easily run into several hundred thousand dollars by virtue of the size of the operation and financial attractiveness of a company with the credit rating of General Electric.

Using only their general market knowledge and sales skills, Robert and Forrest Gibson, one of his young office leasing specialists, had mesmerized the local management of GE, beating out their many competitors for the exclusive right to represent them in the new lease negotiations. Robert was no fool, and quickly realized what President Clinton had meant when he said that winning is sometimes like the dog finally catching the truck. What do you do with it now that you've caught it?

Much of my professional time over the previous ten years had been spent in the negotiation of major office leases in markets as diverse as New York, Los Angeles, Toronto, and Brussels. I knew from an abundance of experience that the process Robert had committed to on behalf of General Electric was extremely complex, and one small mistake on their part could cost them hundreds of thousands of dollars in commissions. Negotiating with Robert had become a high wire act, in that I knew he needed me very badly for this one deal that could prove to be one of Jacksonville's largest, but at the same time I had to steer clear of controversy due to my ongoing fear of having the debacle in Houston come with me to Jacksonville.

The original hope of total anonymity in this new market over a thousand miles from Houston had died a violent death before we ever moved. During one of the house hunting trips provided by the foundation, I had arranged to interview with each of the top five local brokerage operations. The very first meeting of the day was with a former Cushman & Wakefield office, now independent and known as Summit Commercial Properties. Summit's president, "Corky" Smith was an extremely knowledgeable and personable man who had decided to make a preemptive strike to keep me from working with anyone but him. He made it clear within the first thirty minutes that he wanted to do whatever was necessary to insure my affiliation with Summit. It was too early to commit and my schedule was tight, so after an hour and a half of intense conversation I tried to excuse myself. At that point Corky got a pained look on his face, and asked something that had been on his mind from the start.

"How did a nice guy like you get tied up in Eternal Values?"

It took every bit of ten tough years of playing financial poker in the big leagues to hide the sinking feeling in my soul. It was as if a trap door had been opened, and a bottomless dark pit awaited. Again.

Sitting back down, mainly to keep from falling, I walked him through the entire sequence of events with special emphasis on the libel suit. I told Corky that he was certainly welcome to a copy of the deposition of author Catherine Chriss stating clearly that there was no reason to believe that I was or ever had been a "neo-Nazi faggot from outer space," my honorary title bestowed by Houston's morning radio show hosts. Corky appeared to be convinced, and all of his subsequent actions have proven him to be as honorable as my first impression.

It was still a shock to know that the story had arrived before I did.

"How did you find out?"

"Before we spun off from Cushman & Wakefield, I had been on the team to consider buying the Horne Company in Houston. When I saw that you had started there, I picked up the phone and called Howard Horne?"

"What did Howard say?"

"He said you had a lot of success and was really shocked to read the story. But he would hire you back in a minute."

The good news was that Howard Horne, son of the founder and chairman of the most successful private brokerage operation in the country thought enough of my character to stand up for me. The bad news was that like almost everyone else in Texas, he had obviously believed the allegations to have some validity. The really bad news was that the story was already in Jacksonville.

It was difficult to muster the strength to go on to the next appointment, but I really believed Corky would hold the information in confidence. Time did prove that he was a man of his word. Unfortunately, time would also prove that not everyone in the Jacksonville brokerage community was of such noble character.

*****

Much of my time at Robert's Atlantic Commercial Properties was spent fulfilling the training requirements of a consulting agreement we had designed to bring some of my expertise to his young company. It had always been difficult for me to take my accomplishments in business seriously, especially when living with a scientific genius whose expertise often saved dying children. The first few training sessions for Atlantic made it clear to me that although Robert had a group of bright and motivated people, Jacksonville as a whole was living in the Ice Age when it came to professional brokerage expertise. His staff listened closely and really wanted to increase their knowledge. That was as much as I could ask. Robert let me know when we discussed their high level of concentration that a good portion of the attentiveness was attributable to my having already repeatedly done what all of them aspired to do, i.e., make several hundred thousand dollars a year while working twenty to thirty hours per week. Many people aspire to productivity as opposed to activity, but they had realized that I actually understood the difference.

Working with Robert and Atlantic slowly rebuilt my confidence to the point that by the time we needed to have face-to-face meetings with the owners of prospective projects on behalf of General Electric, I was not only ready but almost excited about getting out again.

As part of my personal preparation for return to activity, I told the brokers at Atlantic in one of our classes that a highly useful element of successful commercial brokerage is mastery of a technique known as the "theatrics of client representation." Brokers, like apes in the wild, actually get mileage out of beating their chest, throwing shit (usually figuratively), and doing other ape-like things to let the little apes know who the big apes are, and therefore that the big apes expect to be treated with big ape respect.

In every meeting during our tour day, Robert made a point of personally introducing me to the land or building owners, covering enough of my success and experience to intentionally send some level of fear into their representative agents. Said another way, Robert was using the GE transaction to let his competitors know that there was a 10,000 pound ape in town now, and that ape was hanging out in the trees with his apes.

The day progressed very well until we came to the last, and presumably most important, appointment. Gran Central Corporation is arguably the finest developer of suburban buildings in Jacksonville, and perhaps in all of Florida. They are a subsidiary of Florida East Coast Railroad, which is, in turn, a subsidiary of the St. Joseph Paper Company. The stock of St. Joseph is held primarily by the Nemours Foundation. Suddenly I found myself in the presence of Jack Dyer of Gran Central -- a direct conduit to the board of my wife's foundation. It was no time for controversy.

Like many institutional developers that are oriented to creating rather than marketing office buildings, Gran Central hired commercial brokerage firms to lease their projects instead of hiring their own sales people. I was surprised to learn that Gran Central had retained CB Commercial (Coldwell Banker) to lease their new project in suburban Jacksonville. Having worked with virtually every brokerage operation of any size at one time or another, I had entrenched predispositions about the general quality of most. CB Commercial was not my favorite, and Robert told me their hyper-aggressive approach and disregard for genteel Southern business ethics had created a number of enemies among the local brokerage community.

CB's on-site agent for the Gran Central project was Maggot. Maggot said very little as we talked with Jack Dyer about the market, Gran Central's objectives with regard to ownership, and the process we were undertaking on behalf of General Electric. Gran Central's building, directly across the street from a major regional mall, was clearly a front runner for the deal. GE's management had already looked at and liked the project.

Our meeting was going smoothly, Dyer was open and personable, but most of the talking was left to me. I seemed to notice Maggot becoming uncomfortable, but making people like Maggot uncomfortable was part of my job. He was straight out of central casting for big company brokers -- GQ suit, blow-dried puffy hair, and really shiny shoes. If he could not yet afford a BMW you could bet that it was on the list of goals in his management-by-objective folder. Even though they looked nice, most of his genre were unable to tell you the difference between the net present value of a cash flow and hair mousse tax calculation. I decided early on to simply write him off as another in a long series of nonentities, succeeding by virtue of his company's sign in front of a building that would lease quickly with or without him.

Gran Central was our last meeting of the day, and as we drove back to the Atlantic office Robert and Forrest both commented on how uncomfortable Maggot had been. Over the past few years, CB had, at least with regard to volume of business, come to be known as the preeminent office leasing firm in town. As far as they were concerned the office market belonged to them. Unknown to me they were also willing to go to unusual lengths to defend their position.

* * * * *

The next morning, I was sitting in my office at home working through the tenth or so revision of a book proposal about Doug Wyatt's cult, the Eternal Values. Before leaving Houston I had spoken to Mike Doran, a local literary agent. He had thought that there might be a tremendous opportunity in the wake of the FBI and ATF fiasco with the Branch Davidians in Waco, Texas. With Mike's assistance, I had set out to write an intelligent book about modern cults in America, with special emphasis on their recruiting processes. It was my first encounter with the world of professional agents, and the continual flow of red ink onto what I had thought was pretty good material had begun to demand large quantities of time for revision. But with my income cut by eighty percent I was flexible.

My digital pager hummed shortly before ten o'clock, and the dial indicated that it was the office of Atlantic Commercial Properties. They called frequently, an understandable annoyance in that the General Electric deal was one of the biggest they had ever controlled. Forrest Gibson was especially sensitive about the deal since he was the father of two young children and GE was his primary hope of a big paycheck in 1993.

Atlantic's receptionist answered, as usual, on the first ring. I had begun to like some aspects of the military influence in business. Kelley always insisted on chatting for a moment when I called, and she had proven to be one of the most interesting people I had met in Jacksonville. Underneath her quiet and professional exterior, she had a past that could easily surface in a Jimmy Buffet bar song. Today though, there was no room for frivolity.

"Good morning, how . . ."

"Robert is standing right here waiting for you. He's walking back to his office."

Robert must have sprinted to his office, and he was out of breath when he picked up the receiver.

"Roger, we've got a real problem."

"What do you expect, it's an ugly business?"

My attempt at humor got no response.

"I've got Forrest here in my office. I'll put him on the speaker phone."

As in most tense situations, Murphy's law took effect and we were disconnected. I called right back, and they were waiting.

Forrest spoke first.

"Roger?"

"Another screwed up real estate deal, huh?"

His voice was shrill: "I was hand delivering the requests for second proposal just like you said and ran into Maggot in the CB Commercial office downtown."

"Did he get the idea that maybe we knew a bit more than he did?"

"He must have, because they are trying to cut your

throat."

Due to the large amounts of personal income involved, commercial real estate brokerage was always intensely competitive. I assumed that it was just another case of an overly sensitive broker being badgered by a jealous competitor.

"So what did the intellectual giants at CB have to say about me?"

There was no way to have anticipated his response.

"I was standing in the reception area talking to one of their guys about the GE deal. Maggot walked out and started laughing at me. He said 'Well, we've got the goods on your new hot shot from Houston. What a prize! This guy's a Nazi and a cult member. Likes little boys, too. We're going to get this article they faxed to us from the Houston office to the *Jacksonville Business Journal* and stop this son of a bitch before he gets started here."

I simply began to fall out of control. There was nothing to say.

Robert finally broke the silence.

"Roger, this is Robert. What the fuck is Maggot talking about?"

For the first time, it became clear to me that Robert had not read the materials I had mailed to him on the libel suit before ever moving to Jacksonville.

"Did you read 'Roger's Story'?"

"I skimmed it. My wife read it. She thought it was really

creative."

Not only did he have no idea of the debacle, his wife had thought my written record of it to be fiction. In what had become commonplace since the onset of clinical depression and my ingestion of massive quantities of antidepressants, I drifted off. Perhaps it <u>was</u> all fiction. Maybe I was just the hapless protagonist in the world's longest tragic comedy. Somewhere out there, Kurt Vonnegut was bouncing me off the interior walls of his word processor like a human racquetball and stoned college students were laughing hysterically with every new calamity.

The trip into mental hyperspace took only a few seconds, and I remembered that the phone was in my hand. I remembered who was on the other end, and why.

"You need to read it, Robert. This whole thing was sent to you before we ever began to negotiate."

"What is this article Maggot is talking about?"

"I'll bring you a copy first thing in the morning, along with the deposition of the woman who wrote it."

"You know that I have to be really careful with the reputation of this company."

"Sure. I'll see you first thing tomorrow."

I was off again to hyperspace in preparation of more Vonnegut material for the stoned kids at school -- accused neo-Nazi faggot from outer space enlightens decorated military officer on recruitment by international cult of wealthy psychos, and his resulting death from friendly fire for blowing the whistle on them. That should have them rolling in the aisles for weeks at the all-night donut shops.

There was barely enough energy in my hand to push the hang-up button on the phone. CB had cleanly and fatally sent an arrow straight into my heart, and there was nothing for me to do but watch for a few beats until all the blood was gone. A year of psychiatric care, God knows how many bottles of antidepressants, constantly walking through psychological super glue while trying to build a new business, and all through it putting on a happy face to hide the mess from my children had just gone straight to hell because a blow-dried yuppie was afraid a serious competitor had moved onto his turf.

The ramifications of Maggot's action came clearly into view. The representative of Gran Central, Jack Dyer, had probably already been given a copy of the article. After uprooting ourselves and our children, and moving a thousand miles to get away from the article, the most widely read business publication in the area was going to print what the board members of the Nemours Foundation might already have been told. They had to be one of the most conservative groups of human beings ever assembled and were going to learn that they had hired a pediatrician with impeccable credentials, excellent references, and a husband who was a woman-hating, psychedelic drug abusing, neo-Nazi homosexual from outer space. We still had a substantial monthly payment on the house we had bought, and lots of credit card debt from the move, and I had no real hope of income anywhere near the established levels of my past. My guess was that they would not fire Shelly, but instead employ a tactic prevalent in most major companies when an employee becomes a problem, i.e., make her miserable enough to quit.

What about the parents of my children's friends? People who had known me for years in Houston had believed the article and given me no chance to tell the truth before barring my kids from their playmates. Here in the deepest of the Deep South, there was no way to envision the potential response toward a homosexual Nazi who had stood on the same YMCA soccer field with their children.

The Colt .380 was still in a locked briefcase in my office closet. I got it out, and laid it on the table in front of me. It sat there for over an hour while I just drifted and stared. Previous experience had convinced me that suicide was cowardly in the light of day but there was no light where I was on this day.

For God knows what reason, all the care of Dr. John O'Donnell, the psychiatrist who would later die of AIDS, kicked in at once. Years may pass before I fully grasp the irony of facing death twice as the result of untrue allegations, only to be saved by a gentle man who in reality was probably many of the things they had accused me of being. In the end, the reality for me was that the mighty and respected tormented me with no opportunity for argument, and the leper saved my life.

As he had taught, I forced myself to think of the other

victims of suicide. I would be out of the pain, but where would that leave the three people who were closest to me? Shelly would be left alone in a strange and suddenly hostile environment with two children who had just lost their best friend.

I put the Colt on safety and took it back to the lock box. It never left the box again while I owned it.

When I called her, Shelly tried to put up a brave front but it was obvious that her worst nightmare had come true. It was all starting again. She had ten patients in the waiting room and had to go.

The lunacy of self-imposed demise was gone, but I was actually lower than when it all began. Still moving in slow motion, a transformation began within me that morning that would dramatically alter my life.

As a child, one of my favorite games was to stick my finger into the *Bible* at random, ask God to say something to me, and then read the passage my finger had fallen upon. In personal validation of psychological studies that claim we revert to childlike behavior during periods of great stress, I did just that for the first time in probably thirty years.

My finger had fallen to the words of the Apostle Paul in I Corinthians 8-12. Paul had always been one of my favorite characters in Christianity, having been quite a hellraiser prior to being sequestered by God on his way to Damascus. This is what Paul said to me: "We are hard pressed on every side, but not crushed; perplexed, but not in despair; persecuted, but not abandoned; struck down, but not destroyed. We always carry around in our body the death of Jesus, so that the life of Jesus may also be revealed in our body. For we who are alive are always being given over to death for Jesus' sake, so that his life may be revealed in our mortal body. So then, death is at work in us, but life is at work in you."

I lay down the *Bible* and picked up my *Bhagavad Gita*. My finger fell to a passage in which the warrior Arjuna was being chastised by Lord Krishna for being unwilling to fight. As Arjuna surveys the armies arrayed for battle, he sees that members of his own family and his closest friends will die in the coming conflict. As a sensitive man as well as a maharatha[5], he feels the strength created by the justice of his cause evaporate into a desire only to slip away into silent exile. In a truly magnificent section of ancient text, Krishna reveals to Arjuna every secret of life, including the reason for death and rebirth -- finally allowing Arjuna a glimpse of the full glory of God. As it would have been for any mortal, the experience was terrifying. As Arjuna implores the Lord to forgive him for his lack of respect, he asks for direction in the attempt to atone for his lack of humility. Krishna instructs him to act like a man and simply play out his role in a story that had already been decided and recorded long ago.

---

[5] Maharatha (Sanskrit) -- A warrior able to single handedly defeat ten thousand archers.

This child's game had a powerful effect. Everything about the way I reacted to the defamation changed in an hour's time. Under no circumstance would I let these people, or anyone else, continue to perpetuate the lie that hounded my family. Killing myself would hurt my family, but not them. Cowering would hurt me, but not them. Hiding in fear could obviously not protect me, and would allow them to go on to damage others.

Sensing an inner strength of boundless dimension, I girded myself for war.

The Hearst Corporation, its *Houston Chronicle*, and their paid by the hour whores in the legal profession cared nothing if I lived or died. They were willing to use lies and collaborate with criminals to win rather than simply publicly admit a mistake their author had already admitted in deposition.

Now a man who knew nothing of me and my family was willing to destroy all of us in order to better his own position in a small-time commercial real estate market.

If all these were willing to torment us with no justification and no remorse, they had just placed themselves on a field of Armageddon of their own creation. On that day I knew the odds and learned the outcome. All that was left was to play out my role. Before ordering my lawyers to rain fire on the heads of CB Commercial and Maggot, I wrote the following poem in an attempt to record what had happened to me that morning:

Armageddon

green pastures
waters still
soul returning
iron will.

enemies wonder
evil moon?
no surrender
destruction soon.

angels gather
horses fly
table spread
bloody sky.

heavens darken
mariah swells
clouds boil
final knell.

steed approaching
rider dark
head exposed
sixes mark.

closer now,
eyes ablaze
valley quiet
siren gaze.

never blinking
piercing me
eyes reveal
evil sea:

dying children
burning men
vampire mothers
cobra den,

killing babies
fanning greed
filling needles
rivers bleed.

fear surrounds
vision gone
angels vanish
left alone.

soft recital
promise made
light returns
shadows fade.

final battle
lies within
only weapon
trusting Him

The *Houston Chronicle* had published the Eternal Values story as a personal favor for a cocaine-trafficking, money-laundering criminal. The favor had ruined my business, humiliated my family, and driven me into the hands of a psychiatrist for treatment of clinical depression that resulted in my five year old seeing a cocked and loaded Colt .380 rammed into the back of my throat. Their way of apologizing was to argue that it was their Constitutional right to do so.

And now the evil had followed me to a new home. I was finally enraged to the point of having every bit of the self-pity and fear that had been my constant companions consumed in the white flame of internal rage. For the first time I was completely prepared to do whatever it took to make it stop.

Cottonmouth was out of town but by the end of the day, Coachwhip had faxed letters to the top officers of CB Commercial, the *Jacksonville Business Journal*, and the *Florida Times-Union*, Jacksonville's daily newspaper. In it he informed them that the untrue allegations of the *Chronicle* article were the basis of a major libel suit, and that the transmission or further publication of libelous information was itself libel. Any rebroadcast of the information about me that was already documented as false would be followed immediately by the most rigorous imaginable protection of my rights. I took his letter, wrote a cover for it, and had a courier take it to the manager of every major brokerage and development company in Jacksonville, including Jack Dyer of Gran Central Corporation.

It has now been over a year since the day of my internal transition, and not a word has appeared in any Florida publication. The once vocal agents of CB Commercial are silent.

Frederick von Mierers had closed each of his audiotapes, even those subliminally indicating that the Holocaust was good, with "God bless you all Christians, Jews, Muslims, and Hindus." As a brilliantly lethal blend of good and evil, Frederick's teachings were as contradictory as his life. Intending to recruit me for his cult, thereby starting me on the same winding road to Hell that he and his followers had chosen, he had unknowingly set me on a path that would this day result in having an internal strength unlike any I had ever known.

I have not once been afraid, ashamed, or indecisive since that day. The journey that began that morning would lead to demanding and getting the attention of the Attorney General of the United States, to exposing the money laundering lawyer responsible for all the trouble, firing my original lawyers and overcoming their sabotage attempt, and down a hundred other paths I never could have imagined.

My battle position became that the things said about me were simply not true. They never had been true. There was no need to know anything else. If the system of justice in America had disintegrated to the point where truth had no relevance, then the system itself would also be my enemy. If the defense tactic of choice was to crush me by virtue of their size and wealth, I would find something bigger and more wealthy to crush them.

My decision to go on the offensive was made logically. The painful ramification was knowing that my children had already been the subject of death threats by Doug Wyatt's cult in retaliation for my exposing them. Now I had made the decision to take on one of the most powerful men in Texas. My friend Bob Goldstein had already warned me that Cobra's friends in the cartel lost no more sleep over hiring professional killers than they did about supplying crack cocaine for use by elementary school children.

The only way to quell my fear and feeling of guilt over further endangering my family was to convince myself that if they hurt my kids they damned well better have killed me first. After twenty-five years of refusing to own a gun, and then buying one only for suicide, I spent my first infusion of company revenue in Florida on an AR-15 assault rifle, a short-barrel Mossberg twelve-gauge shotgun, and a Smith & Wesson .45 automatic pistol equipped with a laser scope under the trigger for nighttime efficiency. I made friends with a neighbor who was a member of the first U.S. Navy S.E.A.L. team, and who now trained new S.E.A.L.s in the delicate art of underwater demolition.

Every day came to include time for target practice, ultimately leading to the day when I could roll down a hill, jump to my feet, and consistently put six out of seven hollow point bullets into a hanging plastic milk jug filled with cat litter fifty yards away.

In order to overcome fear, I chose to confront my lifelong paranoid fear of snakes. Our new home sat on a river teeming with Eastern cottonmouths that often reached seven feet in length. I began to hunt them, shooting them at first with the shotgun, then a pistol, and ultimately capturing them with a homemade snake stick. While they struggled in the loop of braided nylon rope I would strangle them with my free hand.

I spent an hour a day on a Stairmaster set at high speed, and another hour lifting weights.

My children and I took martial arts training together, and I broke my toes repeatedly practicing kicks on an Everlast bag. As preparation for a night attack by a hired killer, I learned to throw Gil Hibben knives accurately and silently in near total darkness. I slowly conditioned myself to wake at irregular intervals in the night, dress without waking my wife, and silently patrol the area around the house. Eventually I was able to move in the night without arousing our three dogs, or those of the neighbors.

* * * * *

Nothing had changed about the way I wanted to be. I could never bring myself to intentionally kill a deer, a duck, or even a nonpoisonous snake. The thought of killing another human being, even one hired to kill me or my family, made me ill. So I thought of the constant preparation only as a chess game with my own conscience, hoping it would never be more.

Even with all the training, my chances against a professional hit man working for a cocaine cartel were poor at best. But at least I could make it a contest if they came when my family was home. If they came for me alone, I was living on borrowed time anyway.

John Lennon was still my only real hero. Nonviolent confrontation was still the best solution to any conflict. But the decision to be aggressive in no longer tolerating humiliation had brought with it a heavy burden of responsibility. I bought the movie *Under Siege* and watched the combat scenes over and over in slow motion while doing my hour a day on the Stairmaster. The lethal confidence of Stephen Seagal ultimately came to be an unexpected addition to the passivity of John Lennon as a part of my personality.

Author's Note

Chapters eight and nine were the last to be written. It is certainly true that we tend to delay most what we like to do least. After avoiding the task for several weeks following completion of the rest of the book it occurred to me that the story regarding the darkest days of my experience in the aftermath of September 1, 1991 had already been written -- in the form or my correspondence during the period. It would be impossible (and psychologically imprudent) for me to have tried to duplicate the emotion of the period between Thanksgiving 1992 and June 1993 without heavy reliance on existing material.

Sold Out

"My daddy is a movie actor, and sometimes he plays the good guy, and sometimes he plays the lawyer."

Malcolm Ford -- Son of Harrison Ford, to his preschool classmates on what his father does for a living

"If I had to choose between betraying my country and betraying my friend, I hope I should have the guts to betray my country."

E.M. Forster, <u>Two Cheers for Democracy</u>

The final chain of events in this story began with a phone call from my attorney, Cottonmouth, to the offices of Atlantic Commercial Properties. I was attempting to standardize their approach to market segmentation in pursuing clients for the office leasing program. It was going well, as those things go, and it allowed me to do something productive in the company of people with whom I had become comfortable rather than have to risk further defamatory attack by CB Commercial or some other competitor in the marketplace.

Cottonmouth was handling some of the ongoing clean-up

of shutting down the old company, including trying to recover the value of some office furniture Scorpion had sold at a fire sale price to a friend of his -- only to pocket the money. I had been expecting a call but not the call I got.

"I guess we should start by me telling you of my decision to leave the firm and take a job in the State Attorney General's office."

It was a two-edged sword. On the one hand, Cottonmouth had by all accounts done a good job to date. The *Chronicle* was leaning backward, if not entirely on the ropes -- an amazing state of affairs for a libel suit. On the other hand, he was a fascinating man intellectually but had told me some things in confidence about his personal life and substance abuse habits that were a bit disturbing as we headed toward trial. His wife's illness had created a combination of economic and personal stress that could well make him ineffectual at just the wrong time. His decision to leave seemed to make good sense for him in that he would have a stable income and probably excellent benefits at a time when security was needed most. Finally, his departure would allow me to be more aggressive in forcing the issue he had always blocked -- criminal activity on the part of Cobra.

We talked for over an hour and left it that he would endeavor to select an attorney to take his place from outside the firm since there were no other members of Coachwhip et al. professionally capable of handling the suit. He would have my support in trying to hang on to a reasonable share of whatever settlement or award might be obtained regardless of who took over for him.

It sounded good, but very early into the replacement process I became painfully aware of the economic reality associated with personal injury legal work. That is, if you can make millions of relatively easy dollars representing people who break their backs at work or get hit from behind in car wrecks, why would you waste your time working on a defamation case that pits you and your client against not only the defendant but the law? The statistics regarding a plaintiff's chances in defamation alone are enough to scare all but the most proficient of experts in the area away forever. Therefore, attempting to sell a case that has been handled by another lawyer who the big time litigators do not feel comfortable with is next to impossible.

Coachwhip finally presented me with two recommendations. I told them from the start that I would be pursuing other options as well. Things were fine until Coachwhip began to feel that his firm really might not retain control of the case. The events that followed are best left to the actual correspondence of the time, beginning with my concern over the handling of crucial deadlines in the wake of Cottonmouth's departure.

The only formal activity Cottonmouth and I had to take together was an appearance at the surprise deposition of Cobra by the *Chronicle* attorneys. There was no reason for them to have called him to testify at all, much less at what was still an early point in discovery. It was not until I was in the room with him that the greatest set-up of my life became clear. It was old home week for Cobra and Hog-nose. Cobra lied from the beginning to the end -- each lie meticulously designed to aid the *Chronicle*. And my lame duck attorney sat passively throughout, not even feigning a defense. At one point I was so furious that we went outside the conference room where I asked him what the hell he was doing -- and then demanding that he ask Cobra questions about his memory of the prior depositions in the *Wyatt v. Sakowitz* suit. He said he would. I also wanted him to document my letters in the court record about Cobra's criminal behavior, thus forcing them to either admit they were using a criminal to aid their cause or dispute the charges so we would have a reason to proceed with formal notification of appropriate parties for the criminal justice system to investigate. Cottonmouth did neither. A letter from the time documents the experience.

* * * * *

January 5, 1993

Mr. Bob Goldstein
The St. James
Houston, Texas

Dear Bob:

I hope that you and Susan are doing well. Things are almost

certainly better for you than Bud Adams -- another case for the theory that money won't fix everything.

Cobra recently gave his deposition in my suit against the *Chronicle*. I thought it interesting that they deposed him instead of us, and a few minutes into the process it was clear why they had done so. He lied from start to finish. He refused to admit things that had happened, and freely created stories to benefit the *Chronicle* that were outright lies. His testimony is potentially devastating to the suit. In some ways, Cobra has taken freedom from both of us.

The most amazing part of the experience was looking straight into his eyes as he performed as a paid whore for the enemy. Most people can't look you in the eye when they are lying. Cobra seemed to feed off the hate and disbelief in mine. The experiences of all these events has left me convinced that absolute evil does exist. It does not belong to races or groups of any kind, but dwells very close to the surface in some individuals. Cobra is living proof.

The only thing Cobra can't take from me is my family, all of whom are doing well. Should he or his friends ever choose to do so, I thought you might enjoy the enclosed fictional account of things that happen to people who cross the line.

Maybe we should start a club or something. . .

* * * * *

After Cobra's deposition Cottonmouth vanished, and my phone calls to Coachwhip et al. were at first slowly returned and then hardly returned at all.

What should have been an orderly process of transition had become an emergency. I had no idea what my lawyers were doing, but it certainly did not appear to be in my interest. After several demands, Coachwhip's office forwarded court documents to me that showed we were in danger of missing deadlines and forfeiting rights at trial -- the kind of mental mistakes made by the opposition that we had repeatedly used to our benefit in the early going.

Whatever was going on, it was time to stop it.

* * * * *

Realizing from the start that the claims I would ultimately make would require substantial documentation, the trail of letters that would stretch across America began.

* * * * *

February 13, 1993

Dear Coachwhip:

When I called you on Friday, and Diamondback intercepted the call, some issues came to the front regarding my suit against Catherine Chriss and the Hearst Corporation that I feel need to be addressed:

> You and the firm were aggressive about taking my libel suit in the first place.

Our contract specifically notes that you endeavor to provide the highest quality legal services.

Until I hear otherwise from an expert on defamation actions, I will continue to believe that your Cottonmouth was capable of providing high quality legal services.

This is a suit with very high dollar value, as evidenced by your own demand letter.

I was continually led to believe that although libel is hard to win, we were making significant progress, especially in light of the conspiracy theory regarding the manipulation of the Chronicle by Cobra.

The departure of Cottonmouth from the firm was a total surprise to me.

By your own admission, the firm does not have anyone else capable of providing "highest quality legal services" on this case.

The two attorneys referred by you to me are not experienced in the very specific area of defamation, were not committed to taking the case to trial and appeal if necessary, and specifically refused to take the case under the financial terms of our agreement -- an agreement that was proposed by and written by your firm.

You do not seem to have any more ideas on attorneys to follow through with your firm's commitment to me.

I have been placed in the awkward position of being responsible for finding my own replacement counsel at a time when, as a result of the defamation, I am out of money, seven hundred miles from Houston, and struggling to get some kind of business going here to support my family.

At least one attorney, Mr. Perdue, to whom I was referred

by Richard Mithoff refuses to take any case that has been handled by any other attorney. I hope to find that this is

not a common attitude, especially in light of the fact that I did not choose to change attorneys.

Diamondback referenced that he was "handling" the discovery of my case in the interim, but was unaware of critical issues like the deadline for filing our expert witnesses by March 1. We have already lost advantage in the case by missing a deadline to file suit against additional parties by February 1. My guess is that the lapse of legal services, and resulting inability to potentially add CB Commercial and Cobra to the list of defendants may prove to be a strategic error.

Diamondback seemed to be annoyed by the fact that your firm was responsible for examination of the transcripts of the various tapes, has already asked for two extensions to avoid doing so, and now seems to be searching for a creative way to avoid it altogether. I do not need to be a lawyer to realize that the opposing counsel in this suit took the action of transcribing the tapes for a reason that they perceive to be to their advantage.

In total, I think it reasonable to assume that the commitment to endeavor to provide the highest quality legal services in the most important legal action of my life is not being honored, and could well cost me the case.

I will continue to the best of my ability to find someone to fulfill the obligation left untended by the departure of Cottonmouth. I do not think it unreasonable to expect your firm to avoid serious damage to my chances while I try to do that.

Specifically, please inform the court that Nick Endres of Easley, Endres, Parkhill, and Brackendorff will be my forensic economist. A "to be named" expert in criminal law will be used to explore the potential impact of our knowing that Cobra has a history in trafficking cocaine, and that one way influence is purchased is through the use of cocaine as an incentive for cooperation. I may well be losing ground in the case by coming to this deadline without a lawyer, but really don't know what to do about it at present.

Sincerely,

Roger D. Hall

* * * * *

As expected, Coachwhip was less than pleased with the correspondence but did at least acknowledge the need for deadline response to deadlines. It had become clear to me that my counsel was cooperating with the opposition.

Soon our skirmish became a full-fledged shooting war, in large part because Coachwhip and Diamondback absolutely refused to take on Cobra. Time after time they amazed me with the lengths they went to in avoiding their fiduciary responsibility. They had not anticipated my transition, and had no warning that the depression and pliability with which they had grown accustomed had been replaced by an absolute commitment to avoid being crushed by a criminal and his group of arrogant puppets.

* * * *

February 23, 1993

Dear Diamondback:

Please submit a new set of interrogatories to the counsel for the Hearst corporation and Catherine Chriss. The list of questions is short, and should not require a great deal of your time. The questions are:

> Have any of the past or present employees of the *Chronicle* that were involved in the writing or approval of the article ever been arrested? If so, when, where, and why?
>
> Have any of the past of present employees of the *Chronicle* that were involved in the writing or approval of the article ever been addicted to cocaine, or treated for abuse of cocaine? If so, during what time period? What was their source of the drug?
>
> Other than the previously addressed Media Round Table, each employee should describe in detail their social, professional, or personal interaction with Cobra. The description should include dates of the interaction.

Thank you for your prompt assistance. Please let me know when responses to these questions may be expected.

Sincerely,

Roger D. Hall

* * * * *

Every new attorney considered by me was told early on of my interest in finding out if part of the motivation in doing a favor for Cobra had been drug related. It was not a war that would directly involve Coachwhip's firm, but the opportunity had to at least be kept alive. Many phone calls after my letter, they still refused to respond -- and missed the deadlines for a series of critical issues.

I was completely out of cash, strapped for time, and knew that something ugly was going on. It was time to notify them of my decision to employ the lawyer referred by Aubrey Calvin eighteen months before -- Wayne Paris. The hold up was that Wayne wanted $7500 up front to justify the time necessary to bring himself up to speed. I didn't have $75 much less $7500. Fortunately for me (I thought) the *Chronicle's* lead attorneys, Hog-nose and Pigmy, had decided to form their own law firm. The demands of start up seemed to have slowed them down as well.

Coachwhip became increasingly obstinate to the point where I sincerely believed that my own counsel of record had motivation to destroy the suit. I stepped up my attempts at documentation of the bizarre behavior.

* * * * *

March 8, 1993

Dear Coachwhip:

This is the first time in the years that I have known you that three phone calls have gone unanswered. Therefore, I assume that you are totally overwhelmed, totally disinterested in my suit, or both. It is important that you understand my position on a few outstanding issues so I will communicate in writing, and hope to speak to you as well in the near future:

> We both still stand to gain by your assisting in a smooth transition to new counsel.
>
> Your letter of February 23 was sent by fax to a number where I work only sporadically, and was not followed up by any other means of transmittal. I saw it for the first time on March 5. Until close review this weekend I was not aware that you had threatened to withdraw on March 8 prior to my finding replacement counsel, allegedly based on rights granted in paragraph four of the letter. Not only is that interpretation not in keeping with the paragraph referenced by you, it seems to me to be a written indication of your intent to sabotage the case because I was not going to use one of your two friends as replacement counsel for your attorney who left in the middle of the suit.
>
> You may be absolutely certain that if you withdraw for any reason prior to my formally replacing you I will sue you for legal malpractice and breach of contract for the entire ifteen million dollar value of the suit allocated it by your firm. I will additionally pursue whatever remedies are available through the licensing and regulatory agencies for attorneys in Texas.
>
> Diamondback takes exception to my contention that he is averse to handling the due diligence for the suit your firm committed to undertake, but he still has refused to do it.

This would not seem a strong defense of his position.

For the record, I have asked on multiple occasions that the cocaine trafficking history of Cobra be investigated as it potentially relates to his obvious control over the management of the largest newspaper in Texas. I am deeply concerned about the repeated efforts on the part of your firm to avoid this issue.

When we spoke on Friday, I had not had time to fully understand the implications of your February 23 letter. In a suit where the opposition includes an extremely wealthy defendant, and parties as financially powerful as the Wyatts and Cobras that would prefer it not come to trial, there may be a jury somewhere that would not think it paranoid to wonder about the underlying basis of this incredible reversal of motivation on the part of Coachwhip et al.

I am still quite confident of my ability to produce eye witnesses at trial who will confirm that I was never a others that will confirm that cocaine traffickers can manipulate the headlines of major newspapers at their whim.

The only thing that I want from your firm is fulfillment of the letter and spirit of the September 12, 1991 agreement to assist me. In light of the February 23 letter, it seems I will have to be more aggressive in that regard.

Sincerely,

Roger D. Hall

* * * * *

March 15, 1993

Dear Coachwhip:

I am in receipt of your letter of today. Wayne Paris will be preparing a draft agreement for my review in the next few days. The terms of that agreement will be significantly less attractive for me financially than those of the agreement you are threatening to breach.

Although I am not an attorney, years of negotiation have taught me that it is less expensive financially and emotionally to walk away than fight when relationships reach the level of ours at this point. I intend to proceed in good faith in my attempts to replace you with Wayne Paris. However, it may be later than March 29 before I can put together the cash for his retainer. If you feel that my threat is so hollow or the potential malpractice case so weak that you run absolutely no risk in following through with filing the motion to withdraw on or before March 29, then you clearly have no reason not to do so. Otherwise, I would suggest that you reconsider the unilateral breach in favor of trading a few weeks for a battle.

In my conversations with Wayne today, he continues to be quite concerned about the now passed March 1 deadline for naming experts. Please consider this to be my third written request for confirmation that your firm met that deadline. Your performance on this issue is of great concern to my potential replacement for you.

Sincerely,

Roger D. Hall

* * * * *

The only thing Coachwhip had to do was avoid dropping his firm as my counsel of record until I was able to borrow the money to pay Wayne Paris. However, after my letter of March 15 he became hyper-aggressive about getting away. There were no logical reasons for his rush.

From the beginning Wayne Paris had employed a strict policy of only saying the least he could to me on speculative matters in the interest of avoiding misunderstanding. His years in the United States Attorney's office in Houston had also allowed him to see all manner of strange behavior that was often symptomatic of activity behind the scenes. Even Wayne openly agreed that something very unusual was going on.

I borrowed the money to pay Wayne's retainer, and the files were sent to him from Coachwhip's office. Finally there would be someone in the legal system on my side of this unholy war. My phone conversations with Coachwhip made it even more obvious that he had become a dangerous man.

I had been backed up against the wall, and Cottonmouth's earlier confession to me landed in their face.

* * * * *

April 1, 1993

Dear Coachwhip:

Your letter of March 30 requesting withdrawal did not reach me until this morning. It clearly constitutes breach of contract and your fiduciary duty to me as your client. In addition to an action for malpractice, I will pursue remedy through the Texas Bar Association as soon as feasible.

> Among other major problems, you and your firm:
>
> Solicited me for the role of representation.
>
> Failed to complete tasks as my attorney that were begun by Cottonmouth related to the roll down of my company.
>
> Put pressure on me to accept a replacement offered by you from outside your firm when your guy quit my case in the middle of the suit.
>
> Failed to answer interrogatories, and withheld them from me until it was too late to do a decent job of responding.
>
> Lost materials critical to the suit that were in your custodial care. Specifically, one of the tapes necessary to file responses to Chriss' first set of interrogatories was never found.
>
> Failed to submit information and requests that you were instructed to do (in writing), causing me to miss deadlines that cannot be recaptured.
>
> Persisted in filing a motion to withdraw when you knew that I was diligently pursuing your replacement.

Your firm has clearly destroyed my ability to achieve the $15 million value of the suit you placed on it. Before you do any more damage, I hereby demand that any and all materials related to me, my company, or the suit against Hearst and Chriss be sent to me at my home address immediately. <u>You are clearly being compensated by someone, I hope it is enough to warrant the betrayal of trust.</u>

Sincerely,

Roger D. Hall

c: Texas Bar Association via Certified Mail No. P 121 507 010
400 West 15th, Suite 1500
P.O. Box 12487
Austin, Texas 78711
Attention : General Counsel

* * * * *

The attack was obviously unexpected and according to later reports scared the hell out of Coachwhip. Having set the stage with a bit of carpet bombing, it was time for some real ballistics.

* * * * *

April 7, 1993

Dear Coachwhip:

I would like to document my position on one issue and formally offer you action on two others:

> You quit. Retaining files not introduced to this point in the legal process is tantamount to stealing. You have given yourself the right to create attorney/client confidentiality, only to use it in your defense when you fail to perform.
>
> Your implication seems to be that I am secretly homosexual or bisexual. I hereby offer to submit to any physical examination of any kind that you choose, including testing for the HIV virus to confirm the validity of my repeated claim that the only two boys I have ever kissed are my dad and my seven year old son.
>
> I hereby offer to immediately fly to Houston, and submit to hair sample gas chromatography drug testing with regard to our impending legal malpractice suit. You, Cottonmouth, and the other members of your firm, including staff, are invited to do the same. All testing, analysis, and confirmation will be done entirely at my personal expense, said expense to be guaranteed by personal note.
>
> Sincerely,
>
> Roger D. Hall

* * * * *

I could pass the drug test, and they could not. I knew it,

and they knew that I knew. It was vicious, but they had started the fight. It was going to be a real pleasure to see them try to avoid censure by the Texas Bar for operating as attorneys while under the influence of illegal drugs. If it was a sham on my part, all they had to do was trim a lock of hair, let me spend some money, then sue me for making up so treacherous a lie. Instead they ran scared.

Having stopped at least my own legal counsel from sabotaging the suit for a moment, I turned my attention to the district court and Hog-nose. I wanted him to know in no uncertain terms that his client was heavily influenced in running their business by an international criminal and that some of their management might be involved in criminal behavior as well. The money was on the way to Wayne, and I was ready to blow the lid off this den of snakes. I sent the following letter to the court and copied it to Hog-nose.

* * * * *

April 6, 1993

Ms. Katherine Tyra
District Clerk
301 Fannin
Houston, Texas 77002

<u>Via Certified Mail</u>

Dear Ms.Tyra:

I am in receipt of the Motion to Withdraw filed by Cottonmouth and the firm of Coachwhip et al. in the case of <u>Roger D. Hall, Plaintiff,</u> vs. <u>The Hearst Corporation and Catherine Chriss, Defendants</u>.

Please be advised that I will be replacing them with one of two firms currently under consideration within the next few weeks. Mr. Coachwhip has been put on notice that I expect complete and immediate return of all files related to this case.

The enclosed letter was sent to Mr. Coachwhip's firm, and I will be following through on the actions noted immediately. Should the outcome of these actions confirm the legitimacy of my complaint, I would like to reserve the right to introduce the outcome of investigation at trial.

Finally, one of the individuals that we will produce as a witness at trial has told me on repeated occasions that he is personally witness to the fact that a motivating character in the cause of this suit has been involved in serious and ongoing criminal activity. I would appreciate any information available as to the relevant mechanism for avoiding defamation in sharing this testimony with the appropriate law enforcement agency.

Sincerely,

Roger D. Hall

c: Mr. Hog-nose
    Mr. Coachwhip

* * * * *

Cottonmouth had once described the root of my problems as "country boy Roger comes to the big city," implying that my naivety resulting from being brought up in a community where people did not incessantly try to cut each other's throats was to blame for being ripped off by Doug Wyatt, Catherine Chriss, and all those who followed. Even if he is correct, it is better to be a fool than a participating member of a society that has been reduced to glorification of predatory behavior.

To Cottonmouth's lasting credit, he was right about my ridiculously naive beliefs. Imagine thinking that being able to produce an eyewitness to serious criminal behavior would be important and perhaps even troubling to an attorney. I was even stupid enough to believe that Hog-nose might have taken an oath about supporting the law at some point.

I went to my post office box a week after notifying the counsel for Hearst and the court system of Harris County that my suit involved more than just a civil problem. To my surprise there was a certified package from Hog-nose and Pigmy's new firm. My assumption was that they had covered their ass by notifying me that they and their client had no knowledge of criminal activity -- and demanding evidence of such an outrageous claim.

Instead they had copied me on their notice of a move for Summary Judgment in our suit.

It was too bizarre. They and their client (and later the court) had chosen to totally ignore the most serious claim of the entire affair. Even Frederick von Mierers and his merry band did not sell cocaine to school kids. Eternal Values had nothing on the respected members of the Houston legal community.

In a great lesson about justice Wayne Paris told me that it was fairly common behavior to make such a move when a strong and wealthy party perceived that its opponent was out of money, without representation, and vulnerable. It was nothing more or less than a move to the kill.

Wayne worked quickly and prepared a brilliant response to block the Motion for Summary Judgment in a hearing to be held on June 10, 1993. It was a fact issue, and we had all the facts.

He went to the hearing and fought like mad, but told me that from the minute he walked in the judge was standing on the side of the *Chronicle*. The judges were elected. This one was retired and reportedly sitting in for his daughter-in-law -- who would be relying upon the endorsement of the *Chronicle* at election time for many years to come.

After twenty months of suffering and fighting the judge granted the summary judgment -- giving a total victory to my enemies.

* * * * *

We were taking a brief vacation, corresponding to Shelly's

first continuing medical education seminar. After checking messages and talking to Wayne at a pay phone in Okracoke, North Carolina, I told her that the fight was done.

The partisanship of Texas law was nationally known, but this was much too personal an experience with favoritism. A man who knew nothing about me whatsoever had condemned me to be eternally documented as unable to overcome claims of carrying all the baggage of membership in one of the sickest cults in American history. At least, I reasoned, the judge had sacrificed me for his family.

I couldn't eat and could no longer fight. There was no money and no where to go except an appellate level where my chances were even worse.

All we could do was try to put it behind us and to store the file cabinet full of evidence that had no place in Texas law.

Hunting Snakes

"Even if it seems certain that you will lose, retaliate. Neither wisdom nor technique has a place in this. A real man does not think of victory or defeat. He plunges recklessly towards an irrational death. By doing this, you will awaken from your dreams."

Yamamoto Tsunetomo, <u>Hagakure: The Book of the Samurai</u>

"Never contend with a man who has nothing to lose."

Baltasar Gracian

In order to understand the decision and events that followed the summary judgment and ruling by the Texas Bar Association it might be helpful to review some influences in my life that had played significant roles in forming my approach to conflict and conflict resolution.

* * * * *

When he was only seventeen my father was part of the

Navy's World War II Pacific operations. His stories of removing the charred bodies of Japanese soldiers from bunkers after they had been killed by flame throwers, burying native children who had been tossed into the air and then speared on bayonets in a bizarre oriental game of catch, and seeing teenage Americans lying dead in the sand as crabs roamed in and out of their gaping mouths had seemed to me as a child to be only strange and oddly amusing fairy tales. It was, I reasoned, his attempt at making stories like the ones that Rod Serling created for television. Surely human beings did not really do such things to each other.

My personal education on war would have come in Vietnam. During my senior year in high school the numbers for the draft lottery rolled up and it was clear that my next stop was going to be Saigon. Two months before time to pack my bags the draft was rescinded. So my personal experience with the lengths people will go to for their own benefit would have to come from the justice system.

*****

One of the tragedies of our national disintegration of the family is losing the time-honored tradition of dads teaching their kids how to defend themselves. It is not a tradition that we can ever expect mothers to be enthusiastic about but is nonetheless a reality of existence that my father imparted by way of example.

My dad would go to incredible lengths to avoid conflict. He was deceptive in that his slight physical build belied a career as a championship boxer in the Navy and a physical strength that came from endless days of unloading (usually alone) refrigerators, washers, dryers, and freezers from boxcars as part of his thirty-five-year career with Sears and Roebuck.

One of my most vivid memories from childhood was his coming home early one day scared to death that he was going to be fired for fighting at work. The salesmen at the Sears store in Joplin, Missouri were the upper class. They wore suits and ties, worked in the air conditioning, and most of them drove new cars. The warehouse guys like my dad were the lower class. They were often dirty and soaked with sweat from the physical process of making sure the customers got what the salesmen had promised.

For whatever reason, the biggest guy in the store had made my dad his pet project for entertaining his friends -- especially the women of the accounting and administrative departments. Every time dad would go to the lunchroom or the time clock this guy would be waiting there with a crowd gathered to see the show. He would take my dad's coffee, lunch, or coke off the table and throw it on the floor or in the trash. His physical actions were always accompanied with slurs about hillbillies, white trash, or whatever epithet was available given his limited vocabulary.

My father's primary goal in life was for me to get an

education and break what he always referred to as the "chain of ignorance" of our family. He saved every penny, worked weekends at odd jobs, and never forgot his goal. He firmly believed that for an uneducated guy from the hills of Arkansas his job at Sears was the pinnacle of opportunity. He could not possibly risk losing it.

After almost a year of humiliation and avoidance, it became unbearable. Even refusing to take breaks and eating lunch in the back of empty delivery trucks could not prevent the inevitable confrontation at the time clock.

On the final day the big guy was waiting at the clock with his usual cadre of supporters. He took the time card from my father's hand and spit on it.

"You need to wipe that off."

"Why? Hillbillies don't mind a little sauce, do they?"

"Because if you don't I'm going to whip your ass."

The response was met with hilarious laughter from the crowd.

"You're gonna whip me -- you sow slopping runt."

"That's right."

The big guy smiled back at his friends, pulled his right arm way back, and threw a big, slow haymaker. Dad was two feet below the fist as it sailed by. Coming up from his crouched position he drove a punch into the taunter's chin that came all the way from his ankles. His six foot three, two hundred pound attacker literally came all the way off the floor, flew backward five feet, and collapsed on the polished cement floor with a broken jaw. The fight was over in less than thirty seconds.

They were both sent home, and after staying awake all night worrying dad went straight to the office of the store manager the next morning -- who immediately asked him to close the door. The meeting was no longer than the fight.

"Lester, that son of a bitch has needed what you gave him for a long, long time. I have no idea how you put up with it as long as you did. You are the hardest worker and the best employee I have ever had, but if you ever fight anyone for any reason in my store again I'll fire you on the spot. Now get out of here and go to work."

The big guy was off work for about a week. When he returned his first stop was to the warehouse where he apologized to my dad. They shook hands and were still close friends when he died a few years ago.

* * * * *

My own philosophy of combat was the product of my father's example, learning about bullies, and the experiences of athletics. At the very real risk of sounding like a middle-aged guy reminiscing about bygone glory days please allow me to share a few events in my experience that I believe played significant roles in a seemingly illogical 1993 decision to take the war to one last battlefield before giving up.

From kindergarten through ninth grade I was the geek with black plastic glasses who was usually the only boy to make straight As and spend his school days in accelerated classes. This propensity for academic success, combined with the unintentional social maladjustment that comes from being an only child made me the target of endless taunting from classmates.

My fifth grade teacher was a kind man named Mr. Geary. He also seemed to be bent more toward academics than social skills, and on many occasions he intervened on my behalf when gangs of tough Midwest ten year olds would make me the unfortunate focus of their fun at recess.

There was one kid in particular who had made my life miserable from the very first day in fifth grade. He was a foot taller and twenty pounds heavier than me and had been nowhere near the IQ distribution ceremonies before birth. He took my milk at the first recess, made me sit away from everyone else at lunch, knocked my books to the ground at any opportunity, and even followed me home -- usually pushing and taunting to the delight of his small herd of hangers-on.

Mr. Geary did all he could to help, but no one can be everywhere all the time. The time eventually came when my stomach was knotted and feelings of fear hit every time the bell would ring for recess or lunch.

The big kid had been particularly vicious during lunch

one day -- to the point where I finally just threw my paper sack in the garbage and went outside to look for a place to hide. He and several friends saw me leave and followed. When they found me hiding behind a tree on the playground he did something that led to an incredible surprise for all of us.

He spit in my face.

As the saliva dribbled down my nose something snapped.

I hit him in the face as hard as I could. He stared in disbelief as I hit him again and again. Finally he tried to run but every time he turned I would hit him in the back of the head forcing him to turn back around for more blows to the face. Finally Mr. Geary arrived to stop the fight. We should have both been sent to the principal's office for a week of suspension, but Mr. Geary just sent us back to class. Later in the afternoon I would learn from a girl in my reading section that Mr. Geary had stood on the steps for several minutes watching the fight before coming down to stop it. She told me that he had a big grin on his face. The big kid and I did not become friends, but he never bothered me again either.

It would be thirty-one years before I snapped like that again, but there was no question that the willingness to fight was lurking somewhere in my nature.

*****

The second critical event came during high school. My

father had wanted very badly for me to play professional baseball. From my earliest memories he insisted that we play baseball every night for awhile when he came home. Although still a glasses-wearing geek and not a natural athlete by any stretch of imagination I had managed to become a pretty good second baseman and line drive hitter -- making every all-star team from the second year of farm club through the end of pony league (ages 8 to 14).

Of all things in life, making the high school baseball team was the most important. Success in high school ball meant college scholarships, and college success led to major league contracts. I had it all planned -- and as far as conflict with academic goals, even Harvard and Yale had respectable baseball teams.

What I had not planned was to spend ten days of the summer before starting high school in and out of a coma following surgery to repair Meckel's diverticulum and a resulting intestinal gangrene infection.

When school started in the fall I was five feet five and weighed one hundred five pounds. Tryouts were in three weeks.

The way our coach dealt with cutting people was to post the names every morning of the people who were to go to practice that day. If you no longer appeared on the list it was over for you. I made it to the very last day of posting -- exhausted buy pretty sure that there would be plenty of time to recover while sitting the bench, as most freshmen did.

The list was posted, and my name was not on it. My dad had already told his friends about my success. It was devastating.

* * * * *

After a few days of feeling sorry for myself I asked my dad to get a set of weights for me from Sears. We put them in the basement, and I remember looking at the cold metal bar above me while lying on the weight bench for the first time and deciding to be the strongest person in my high school of fifteen hundred.

By the end of my senior year my best bench press was three hundred fifty pounds -- seventy pounds more than the second strongest guy. My physical size had exploded to six foot one and two hundred ten pounds. I had literally doubled in size during high school. I never played baseball again, but had been all-conference my junior year and all-state as a senior in football. There were lots of academic scholarships coming on an unsolicited basis, but the athletic offers were a disappointment in that major colleges thought me too slow to be a blue chip prospect and offered only a chance to play as a freshman with no scholarship -- but with the hope of winning one for the second year.

Our local college, Missouri Southern had an energetic new coach named Jim Frazier. He was absolutely convinced of his ability to turn a football program that had a history of below .500 performance into one of the premier small college teams in the nation. He was a convincing salesman, and lots of us who would have been borderline candidates at Arkansas or Missouri signed on to his dream.

None of us could have known that his dream would become reality overnight. We won every regular season game in 1972, including some against NCAA Division I teams like the University of Nevada - Las Vegas who had put us on their schedule as whipping boys for their homecoming party. Their newspaper made a big joke of us the day of their game, picking UNLV to win by four touchdowns. They were five short when the final whistle blew.

One of the great things about playing for a small college was getting a significant amount of playing time as a freshman. My real claim to fame was not as a starter on the offensive line but as the designated madman on special teams. I had learned accidentally what so many coaches try so very hard to impart to their young players -- the harder you play the less likely it is that you will be hurt.

For example, my job on the kickoff team was to run full speed down the middle of the field and locate the players comprising what was known as the "wedge." The guys in the wedge were typically the four biggest people on the team and their job was to stay close together while the player fielding the kickoff moved in behind them. They would then plow down would-be tacklers, hopefully creating an open lane for a long return. After locating the wedge, my job was to run to the middle of it and leap sideways into the air in such a way as to arrive at the wedge just about knee-high. Twice during one game against the University of Missouri - Rolla I was able to knock down not only all four blockers but the ball carrier as well.

To the kind of mind that can ascend to the highest court in the land this may well seem a barbaric precursor to suicidal behavior, but the strange reality is that I never once received any serious injury -- and on only one occasion had to recite the multiplication tables all the way through before regaining the ability to remember my name.

The point is that going for broke is not only sometimes a suitable option, it may even be the safest when traveling in hostile territory.

* * * * *

Suddenly a program that had no winning seasons in any living person's memory found itself in the 1972 NAIA national championship game.

* * * * *

The momentum and excitement mounted (Joplin, Missouri, did not have a plethora of great athletic moments) to a frenzy by the end of December in 1972. We were playing Northwestern of Iowa. When they came into the cafeteria for the pregame meal and we looked each other over, it seemed that they had somehow taken the Green Bay Packers and snuck them into a college program for one day. They were so big they obscured sunlight.

It was a good clean game, and the lead changed hands four times. Finally it seemed our dream was to end. We were running out of time, and they were ahead by four points. Our defense stopped them on their own eighteen, and they were setting up to punt. We were no real threat on punt returns, and it seemed like an ideal time to try for a block. That was the decision, but my job was to hold up the offensive tackle at the line of scrimmage for three seconds, then turn back down field to block or cover the ball in case of a fumble. Coach Frazier was a positive man but not one to sell discipline short for anyone. Intentional failure to do your job was very likely to win you thirty days of running four miles after practice with all pads and your helmet on. It might be the last game of 1972, but at the time I was planning on three more years of practices.

With nothing other than instinct to blame I never hesitated when the center snapped the ball back to the punter -- charging outside past the tackle who had set his feet to keep me from going inside. They anticipated a block attempt and had placed three backs between the line and punter as a safety mechanism should any of our players break through.

Northwestern was an impeccably well-coached and disciplined team. They had studied our game films closely, and each of the backs took two steps outward to set themselves in the areas where our attack would most likely surface. None of them expected me to be turning back inside after going around the baffled tackle and heading straight up the middle.

The ball (and unfortunately the punter's foot) had landed in my stomach as I flew into him so I was lying face down in the grass trying to remember how to breathe when the celebration erupted. One of our reserve linebackers had fallen on the ball in the end zone for a touchdown. We won.

* * * * *

So long before the *Houston Chronicle* made me famous as a neo-Nazi pervert from outer space the *Joplin Globe* designated me a football hero.

* * * * *

The credit for 1972 lies entirely at the feet of Jim Frazier. He never allowed us to realize that we had no earthly chance of a winning season, much less a national championship. Coach Frazier was a man of great integrity who would make our lives miserable if we broke the rules or took cheap shots against a team that played by the rules. But time after time he managed to be turning his head to cough at those points in game films where I had found some consistently dirty player on an opposing team standing still around a play before the whistle blew -- and planted him in the grass or astroturf.

* * * * *

And that background leads to an understanding of the final play in this story of my war with the Goliath of news media, their silk stocking attorneys, the Texas judiciary, a cocaine trafficker, and decisions of the Supreme Court gone bad.

* * * * *

Shelly was not thrilled with the decision I was going to make but understood better than anyone in the world I could never live with myself without exhausting the final legal avenue of retaliation -- regardless of how corrupt the system might be.

I borrowed another $3500 and Wayne Paris worked his tail off to prepare our appeal of the summary judgment. While Wayne stuck to playing in the system he believed in, and maintained a level of ethical behavior that contributes to my belief that all hope may not be lost for justice in this country, I set out on my own. Unknown to Wayne Paris, my wife, or anyone else, I had decided to cut outside the tackle and look for an opening up the middle.

The following is a selection of unsolicited correspondence sent by me prior to the appellate hearing.

*****

June 25, 1993

Judge Jack O'Neill
152nd District Court of Harris County
301 Fannin
Houston, Texas 77002

Re: Summary Judgment Rendered in Cause No. 9152328, Roger D. Hall v. Hearst Corporation

Dear Judge O'Neill:

I have continually pondered my course of action since your decision on June 10 to enter a summary judgment in favor of the Hearst Corporation in my libel action. It is finally time to respond.

Your decision was wrong. You took a tiny sliver of information and made a poorly informed unilateral decision to deny me the right to produce volumes of factual evidence (including sworn statements of actual former cult members) as to the true nature of my relationship to Douglas Wyatt and Eternal Values. I was never a member of that cult, a homosexual, a neo-Nazi, or a user of psychedelic drugs.

You have denied me of more than a right to trial, you have denied my children the right to see the truth produced about their father. I have long since foregone interest in monetary damages, and in my once naive belief that an elected judiciary is capable of impartial fairness. However, please be advised that it will be a cold day in Hell when I give up my willingness to fight to make the truth known in this cause of action. Since it is my understanding that you are formally retired, and simply sitting in until your daughter-in-law returns from maternity leave, perhaps you can put yourself in the position of having your grandchild see this article about you when grown, never knowing that it was run in haste as a personal favor to a cocaine trafficker.

I am not afraid of Cobra, his criminal friends, the Hearst Corporation, or anything else. I am not afraid because I am right. The enclosed selection of materials pertaining to a complaint under review by the State Bar of Texas may give you a feeling for the degree of adversity I have overcome to bring the case to your attention at all.

You made an incorrect decision about the most important fight of my life without knowing anything at all about me, and little about the facts. I know nothing at all about you. If you are an honorable man, please reconsider and let me have the only thing that I want -- my day in court. If you are not, do not be surprised to find me digging until I am dead to learn why an elected judiciary in Texas is so protective of big law firms and the press.

Sincerely,

Roger D. Hall

* * * * *

The Texas Bar Association had been consistently proving itself to be as lame as the 152nd district court -- understandable that in a profession of image it was hard to get excited about taking action that might tangentially harm the newspaper.

* * * * *

August 4, 1993

Ms. Elaine Machuga Moore
Assistant General Counsel   <u>Via Express Mail TB208664368US</u>
State Bar of Texas
1111 Fannin, Suite 1370
Houston, Texas 77002

Re: H0049303058 Roger D. Hall - Coachwhip

Dear Ms. Moore:

Please find enclosed my response to your notice of a hearing on August 12, and the request for additional documentation. My letter of April 1, 1993 was copied to the Bar, and has been significantly expanded and supplemented herein. Additional information is included regarding issues raised by Mr. Coachwhip's letter of May 13, 1993. Much of the correspondence included has come from files on the hard drive of my computer. The originals are in the files of my attorney, Mr. Wayne Paris. Mr. Paris has all of the depositions and other documents related to the suit. You are welcome to review any of those materials as well.

It will not be possible for me to attend the hearing on August 12. My lack of interest in attending is outlined in the last section of this response. However, I will be sitting next to my phone, between the hours of 4:00-6:00 CST on that date and will be happy to accept <u>collect</u> calls from you or any member of this process during that period.

Sincerely,

Roger D. Hall

<u>Allegation No. 1</u> -- Mr. Coachwhip solicited me for the role of representation.

Following the *Chronicle* article on September 1, 1991 my business partner was approached by an attorney and friend of his with the firm of McConn and Hardy named Julienne Faustini. Since the article was clearly libel, she gave him a collection of materials on the issue and suggested pursuit of a suit.

I made a series of calls to my friends in the legal community. Aubrey Calvin of the firm of Calvin, Dylewski referred me to Wayne Paris (who is now my counsel in this matter). I called Mr. Paris and arranged a meeting for Thursday, September 12, 1991 at 1:30 p.m.

On Monday, September 9, 1991 Mr. Coachwhip, who had done a small amount of corporate legal work for me in the past called to tell me that he had just retained the services of Cottonmouth, a specialist in personal injury and defamation. I had no specific complaints with the business law performance of his firm, and agreed to meet with he, Diamondback, and Cottonmouth on Wednesday, September 11 at 1:30 p.m. In what I would be willing to swear to as a "hard sell" Mr. Coachwhip insisted that Mr. Paris would not be able to provide the level of service of Cottonmouth due to his lack of defamation experience. An interesting claim in light of the fact that Mr. Coachwhip knows nothing whatsoever about Mr. Paris' background.

Before the end of the day, Mr. Coachwhip had prepared the agreement dated September 12 (previously submitted to the Bar), brought it to me and insisted that my meeting with Mr. Paris be delayed or canceled. My psychological condition at the time did, in fact, create a wish on my part to minimize the amount of time devoted to selection, and I signed the agreement and canceled the meeting with Mr. Paris.

Mr. Coachwhip will undoubtedly contest this version of the story, so I will simply raise the logical question:

"Why would I solicit a real estate and tax lawyer for litigation services when I had access to multiple prominent attorneys in Houston through my involvement as founder of the Drug-Free Business Initiative?"

The logical flaws of Mr. Coachwhip's defense will be a comment theme throughout this discussion.

<u>Allegation No. 2</u> -- Failed to complete tasks as my attorney that were begun by Cottonmouth related to the roll down of my company.

The damage of the *Chronicle* article resulted in a "Hurricane Andrew" effect on my company. Cottonmouth agreed to work on my behalf, and received legal fees for recovery of money owed me regarding sale of my office furniture.

When he announced he was leaving, he simply said he was not going to carry out the tasks he had been paid to do. Mr. Coachwhip said he did not have time to mess with it. The money was never fully collected.

<u>Allegation No. 3</u> -- Put pressure on me to accept a replacement offered by you (Coachwhip) from outside your firm after your attorney quit my case in the middle of the suit.

Mr. Coachwhip's letter of May 13 to Mr. Robago contains a series of blatant lies. A copy of that letter with my notes is included for your review. This allegation is the source of the greatest single number of misrepresentations on the part of Mr. Coachwhip. In the interest of clarity, I would like to offer a series of facts that may give you a better feel for the events surrounding this area of dispute:

1) Cottonmouth's resignation came as a complete surprise to everyone. It is my hope to apply enough pressure to find out

how he was compensated to leave.

2) Cottonmouth's resignation was effective around Thanksgiving 1992. Mr. Coachwhip used four months to get me to invest time and travel expense to meet with two attorneys on different occasions. Mr. Coachwhip claims in his letter to Mr. Robago that he spent six months as my counsel after exhausting all potential replacements. His motion to withdraw was made on March 30, 1993. Mr. Coachwhip's statement does not mesh with the calendar.

3) Attorney A is a very close friend of Mr. Coachwhip. Attorney B is his former partner and still friend. In both cases, Mr. Coachwhip made it clear to me that his motivation was to remain personally involved in the suit, and that this would be most easily accomplished by selecting one of these men to replace Cottonmouth. At the beginning of this process, I contacted an old friend and member of the Board of Directors of my Drug-Free Business Initiative, Bill Shrader of the firm of Horan & Devlin for advice. He made it clear to me that although it would clearly be in the best interest of Mr. Coachwhip to use one of his friends, it would not necessarily be in mine to do so.

In the fewest possible words, I would describe my impressions of the two attorneys presented for consideration as follows. Attorney B is an egomaniac whose main claim to fame as an attorney is in the representation of Mel Powers against his defrauded creditors. Attorney A showed up to our interview in a slick black leather jacket and reptile-skinned boots, informed me that he had never worked on a case involving this magnitude of financial damages, and requested $5000 up front to review the files. In both cases, Mr. Coachwhip's claim that I represented in any way my desire to use either of these attorneys is a blatant lie. My replacement efforts continued, involved four prominent Houston attorneys, and led me back to Wayne Paris. It is my mistake to have failed to heed Aubrey Calvin's advise and referral to Mr. Paris in the beginning. Also with regard to this issue, Mr. Coachwhip accuses me in the letter of May 13 of being unwilling to spend any of my own money in this effort.

Since you have subpoenaed Mr. Paris for this hearing, you might ask him about my willingness to make a personal financial commitment to the suit.

In the letter of May 13 to Mr. Robago Mr. Coachwhip claims that I withheld information and misrepresented facts. These claims are his fundamental justification for withdrawal. Those claims will serve as the core of my impending malpractice and defamation actions against him, but for the time being I would ask the members of this committee two questions regarding this issue:

<u>Mr. Coachwhip had all the information he claims led to his withdrawal for more than a year prior to that withdrawal. Why did he wait so long to fulfill his ethical commitment to his profession?</u>

<u>Why would Mr. Coachwhip refer a hopeless case with a lying, drug addicted plaintiff to his friends?</u>

I have not seen the data presented in the first hearing, but based on Mr. Coachwhip's behavior to date I assume that he has either falsified or misrepresented the medical records of Dr. John O'Donnell. Dr. O'Donnell has now retired from medicine, but I have recently been able to make contact with him and expect to have him appear in the impending legal malpractice proceedings as a witness regarding this issue. For the present investigation, I would like to rest my argument by again referring to the two questions above regardless of what Mr. Coachwhip may or may not have said.

For several months, I attempted to maintain a civil relationship with Mr. Coachwhip. I was struggling to rebuild a business. Part of that rebuilding included assembling the funds to retain an attorney the caliber of Mr. Paris. Eventually, Mr. Coachwhip understood that he would be replaced. This knowledge led to the behavior that created the need for this hearing. A series of unexplained comments and actions on his part gave me concern, but never did I anticipate what became a frontal assault on his part to sabotage the suit. I hope that these facts give the members of the committee adequate reason to believe that what Mr. Coachwhip refers to as "retaliation" on my part in his letter of May 13 is a defense of his attack following acknowledgement of my unwillingness to accept his friends as counsel.

I cannot <u>yet</u> prove what I believe to be true. It will take a break in the facade of either Mr. Coachwhip or Mr. Cottonmouth as they become more concerned about exposure to verify, but I do firmly believe that one or both have been paid to destroy this suit and get me to go away. Mr. Cottonmouth is financially strained from years of low pay at the ACLU and has a sick wife. Mr. Coachwhip is not doing well financially, in part because of his missed projections on the revenue to be created by Mr. Cottonmouth. At least one incredibly wealthy Houston family would like to see investigation about the participation of two family members in a dangerous cult ceased. One wealthy and respected member of the Bar would certainly like to avoid exposure of his criminal activity. A huge corporation with a history of ethical depravity could avoid a potentially massive judgment. It does not take a student of the work of John Grisham or Scott Turow to see a significant financial opportunity for two men in dire financial straits.

In summary, when Mr. Coachwhip and Mr. Cottonmouth finally knew they would not make money working for me, they resorted to whatever means became available to make some.

<u>Allegation No. 4</u> -- Failed to answer interrogatories, and withheld them from me until it was too late to do a decent job of responding.

There will be more inclusions in my malpractice filing, but as an example of documentation for this particular claim is included as my letter of March 24, 1993 to Mr. Coachwhip. He had received a set of interrogatories on November 18, 1992 (prior to the departure of Mr. Cottonmouth). As you can see from the information prepared by me, the responses to these interrogatories are absolutely critical with regard to understanding the transcripts prepared by the counsel for Hearst. The date for response had been missed twice before I found out that the interrogatories even existed. Upon learning of the problem, I demanded to be allowed to prepare the response myself. During a period when I was struggling to create revenue in a new and unfamiliar environment, I was forced to take a full week off to prepare the enclosed <u>twenty-four page response</u>.

<u>Allegation No. 5</u> -- Lost materials critical to the suit that were in your custodial care. Specifically, one of the tapes necessary to file responses to Chriss' first set of interrogatories was never found.

Mr. Coachwhip has already admitted losing a sixty minute tape critical to an interrogatory response. In his response to the Bar he said that he did not believe it was critical. This statement is patently untrue, but more importantly how could he make that statement to you if he never heard the tape before he lost it?

His defense seems to be that we could get a copy from opposing counsel. What kind of message does it send to an adversary in litigation if my counsel cannot even succeed in the task of safekeeping information?

<u>Allegation No. 6</u> -- Failed to submit information and requests that you were instructed to do (in writing) by me, causing me to miss deadlines that cannot be recaptured.

The understanding of the importance of this allegation is critical to my complaint before the Bar. Correspondence is included to document the following historical summary leading to a critical mistake in Coachwhip's representation of me:

1) I first became concerned about the possibility of a drug problem on the part of Cottonmouth as the result of an interrogatory response submitted by the defendants in my suit. An important aspect of libel suits is whether the plaintiff is a public or private figure. When we asked Hearst to present articles validating their claim that I was a public figure, the only

article they could find from Chronicle history was one quoting me as saying that a ruling by the Texas Supreme Court upholding an employer's right to do drug testing was a positive step. In the same article Cottonmouth (then with the ACLU) was quoted as saying it was abhorrent. It was unsettling, but not sufficient to cause me to fire him.

2) The article leading to the libel suit was a favor for Cobra. In her deposition, author Catherine Chriss not only admits that the perception of me created by the article as a drug-abusing, woman-hating homosexual neo-Nazi are untrue, she specifically says that the article was promoted by Cobra. Cobra had spent a great deal of time convincing me that if I would testify as to the nature of Doug Wyatt's cult based on information I had obtained by tracking down his old girlfriend (a former member of the cult) the information would be confidential and not released to anyone outside the parties to the suit and their counsel.

Other testimony offered by Chriss and others confirmed that Cobra had spent years attending a social/professional organization known as the Media Round Table. He had patiently courted the management of the *Chronicle* in preparation for the day when he would need a favor.

3) After being manipulated and effectively destroyed by him, I learned that Cobra had a long history of affiliation with cocaine traffickers and other criminals. During the roll down of my company, an old friend (see Goldstein correspondence) revealed to me that not only had Cobra been personally involved in criminal activity, he (Goldstein) had gone to prison covering up for Cobra in a cocaine conspiracy case.

Upon learning of his character, I immediately sent the enclosed letter to Cobra (who continued to call me repeatedly seeking assistance) telling him that I knew of his past and to leave me and my family alone. Cobra never responded to the correspondence until his deposition in my suit, but did finally stop calling me.

4) For almost two years (November 1991 to June 1993) I

repeatedly engaged in heated arguments with Cottonmouth voicing my opinion that the ability of a felon (Cobra) to manipulate the largest newspaper in Texas to the point of running a front page Labor Day Sunday banner headline story that its competition did not run at all (not newsworthy) was extremely relevant to the case, and would be compelling information for a jury to understand the kind of people we were dealing with in our litigation.

Mr. Coachwhip's response to this issue in his letter to you was pitiful. Mr. Cottonmouth's arguments with me were more compelling. He repeatedly said that if we messed with Cobra we would certainly get sued and probably shot. Cottonmouth had worked with Cobra at the ACLU, and knew him well. With a wife and two small children, I held those arguments to be substantial but not reason to avoid introduction of Goldstein's testimony.

Cottonmouth also repeatedly made the assertion that we could win without stirring Cobra up, and that his decision as my counsel was to avoid "giving Cobra the opportunity to make up creative lies for his friends at the *Chronicle* rather than just getting one of the 'bozos' at the *Chronicle* to admit his involvement."

This issue was always a point of significant friction between myself and Cottonmouth. It became critical when the *Chronicle* deposed Cobra. The move was a surprise, did not make sense at the time they did it, and immediately led us to believe that it was a premeditated and planned move by Cobra and his friends at the *Chronicle* to crush our efforts. Having read the depositions of Lynn and Doug Wyatt in the case of Wyatt v. Sakowitz, I should not have been surprised at how little fear rich people have of committing perjury. There was no way for me to anticipate the lengths Cobra would go to in lying for his friends at the *Chronicle*. He lied about every important issue in the deposition, smiled at me while he did it, and made a bold attempt to discredit the suit altogether. Throughout his deposition Cottonmouth was passive to the point of assisting the opposition. I finally called for a break to take my representative

Cottonmouth out of the room, and demanded that he raise the criminal activity issue to allow us to at least discredit the source of the lies at trial. Cottonmouth refused and responded by ending the deposition. It was like being in a war and having your only ally turn around and shoot you.

Shortly after Cobra's deposition and Cottonmouth's poor performance, Cottonmouth left Coachwhip's firm.

5) Wayne Paris should be willing to testify before you that lack of fear of Cobra was an important criteria for my selection of him as replacement counsel.

6) During the replacement process I learned a few days before deadline that Coachwhip had failed to prepare a critical response naming expert witnesses. As evidenced in the enclosed correspondence I demanded that they inform the court of my desire to produce an expert witness to investigate the drug trafficking history of Cobra, the drug abuse history of *Chronicle* management and staff involved in the article, and hopefully create a scenario whereby someone on the defendant's side would break and admit that part of their allegiance to Cobra was the result of his role as a supplier of drugs. Whether successful or not, given the devastating job of perjury done by Cobra in his deposition had to be addressed, and this was one avenue.

7) I followed my letter up twice on the phone, and was assured by Diamondback (of Coachwhip's firm) that the experts would be introduced.

8) I found out after it was too late that Diamondback had lied to me and not named the experts as promised. This date could not be recaptured and will always be a major detriment to my hopes of recovery.

Allegation No. 7 -- Persisted in filing a motion to withdraw when you knew that I was diligently pursuing your replacement.

After wasting months of my time, Mr. Coachwhip suddenly became extremely aggressive about withdrawing from representation. I was down to two potential replacements, and had effectively chosen Mr. Paris when Coachwhip made his motion to withdraw against my vehement objection. The opposition filed a motion for summary judgment at exactly the time Coachwhip withdrew. My letters document the fear (obviously well founded) that a lapse in representation would be dangerous.

The summary judgment was recently granted by a retired judge sitting in for his daughter-in-law who will be subject to review by the *Houston Chronicle* for years to come. We have appealed, and it will now be much more expensive to get this case to trial. The motion was granted without the knowledge withheld by Cottonmouth and Coachwhip regarding Cobra's manipulation and criminal ties.

It is important to understand that the motion for summary judgment was made by an attorney who not long before had requested mediation. No new information had come to light prior to the motion for summary judgment.

Mr. Coachwhip and Mr. Cottonmouth would have succeeded in the attempt to sabotage the case if it had not been for my partial financial recovery, and their naive belief that I would led them get away with it.

Other Issues

1) Use of Illegal Drugs -- It is my objective to prove in the malpractice action that Coachwhip not only lied but falsified documents. In the interim, this is one of those issues that does not have to be subject to finger pointing. On multiple occasions, as documented herein, I have offered to personally submit to the most accurate form of drug testing known. Gas chromatography testing could literally reveal specific use years in the past. One of the great victories of this exercise to date is the repeated refusal on the part of Cottonmouth and Coachwhip to submit to this testing at my expense. For the last time, I will prepay for the tests, and take mine first.

As founder of one of the most successful anti-drug programs in America, I long held that drug problems like his that Mr. Cottonmouth described to me shortly before his departure were best held in confidence by the employer (or in this case, client), and dealt with by treatment. This seemed to me to be particularly true in this instance since his wife was seriously ill, and that combined with the inherent stress of pursuing litigation as a career. There are, however, lots of people that deal with great levels of stress without resorting to cocaine and other crutches. Mr. Cottonmouth and Mr. Coachwhip did not have to make this problem an issue. They did so of their own free will.

2) <u>Anti-Semitism</u> -- This whole thing started because Doug Wyatt told me that Jews were evil, and that Hitler's program of elimination had to be fulfilled. Depositions support the fact that it was this issue that revealed the true nature of his cult, and opened the door for further examination and exposure. You have previously been presented with witnesses regarding my position, including the past president of the Anti-Defamation league.

You have also been presented with excerpts from my collection of writings known as "353 Letters I Didn't Send" on this topic that Mr. Coachwhip must have forgotten to include in his submission. The entry of a humorous letter that is not anti-Semitic in conjunction with this bold faced lie is a mistake that Mr. Coachwhip will long regret. By the way, I am Jewish.

3) <u>Confidentiality</u> -- With regard to your request for confidentiality, I assume that Mr. Coachwhip and Mr. Cottonmouth are sworn to uphold the law as attorneys. In purchasing illegal drugs, Mr. Cottonmouth has, by definition, dealt with and compensated known felons. As seen in the enclosed materials, he and Mr. Coachwhip have gone to great lengths to withhold information regarding criminal activity. The firm has a history of representation of, and personal relationships with people like Mel Powers. It would not seem to me to make sense to protect these people from law enforcement agencies by withholding the results of these proceedings.

Additionally, I quite honestly believe from my experience in the last three years that although the legal system in Texas is extremely adept at making rules, it has somehow lost its ability to evaluate and administer justice. The truth seems to consistently become mired and then lost in the preservation of legal rules of order. In this case, we have a front page story run as a favor for a criminal. The criminal and his puppets in the media are not only protected by my legal counsel, but by the Texas district courts. To the extent that I truly believe and can verify these claims, do you really expect me to refrain from exposing a system this corrupt to the light of public scrutiny?

4) <u>August 12, 1993 Hearing</u> -- Based on the last three years of my life, I have no faith whatsoever in the fairness or integrity of the legal system in Texas or its membership. Something has gone terribly wrong when it is possible to lie and then hide behind the First Amendment as long as you have lots of money and friends in the judiciary. Something has gone terribly wrong when you can engage in criminal activity, commit perjury with ease, and serve as the right hand to the mayor of the fourth largest city in the United States. Something has gone terribly wrong when legal counsel can hide drug impairment and betrayal of trust behind the Fourth Amendment.

I no longer have much of an emotional attachment to Texas, although it was not that long ago that the Chamber of Commerce called me its "Outstanding Young Houstonian" and my pregnant wife and I drove all night from her father's hospital bed in Missouri because we did not want our only son to be deprived of the right of being a native Texan. I certainly have no opinion of any of you that will read this correspondence.

All I have left is the undaunted belief that I was unfairly and unnecessarily destroyed, and that the system that should have protected my rights is so blind and corrupt that it is useless.

I have no more faith in the State Bar of Texas than in the 152nd District Court that refused to give me a chance to let go of Texas with a clearing of the record. <u>All I want of the State Bar is for</u>

someone to sign for the Express Mail Package so I will have proof that the information arrived.

* * * * *

The State Bar of Texas sent me a letter saying that the behavior of my complaint was outside their jurisdiction -- and no action would be taken.

* * * * *

August 17, 1993
Ms. Elaine Machuga Moore
Assistant General Counsel - State Bar of Texas
1111 Fannin, Suite 1370
Houston, Texas 77002

Re: H0049303058 Roger D. Hall - Coachwhip

Dear Ms. Moore:

Thank you for your prompt written notification that money laundering, acquisition and use of illegal drugs including cocaine, perjury, and betrayal of trust are not outside the ethical boundaries of members of the Texas Bar as recorded in Vernon's Texas Codes Annotated, Volume 3 of the Government Code, Title 2, Subtitle G-Appendix A, Article X, Section 9.

Please provide me with all records pertaining to the above referenced matter as soon as possible. I assume that these records are available to me under the Freedom of Information Act. I will be glad to prepay any related expenses you may incur in sharing these materials.

Sincerely,

Roger D. Hall

c: The Honorable Janet Reno   Via Express Mail TB472688326US
   Attorney General of the United States
   Department of Justice

The Honorable Ann W. Richards
Governor of Texas   Via Express Mail TB472688337US
P.O. Box 12428
Austin, Texas 78711

* * * * *

The State Bar refused to release the hearing records to me. Having failed to find an honest person in the Texas Bar I decided to look elsewhere.

* * * * *

November 5, 1993

The Honorable Janet Reno
Attorney General of the United States
Department of Justice
Tenth and Constitution Avenue NW - Room 4400
Washington, D.C. 20530

Dear Attorney General:

In follow up to my correspondence of August 17, 1993, I would like to make you aware of the oral argument date for my appeal in the libel suit against the Hearst Corporation. I do not want any help from anyone in supporting my position, but would specifically ask for your attention to what I feel is an effort by the Texas judiciary to keep me from having the opportunity to do so.

Unless the First Amendment has been expanded to protect the right of criminals to manipulate management of the press to the point of having virtual control over the front page of the largest newspaper in Texas, I continue to feel that light needs to be shed on this case.

Thank you for your consideration, and for any support you might be able to lend.

Sincerely,

Roger Hall
P.O. Box 638
Middleburg, Florida 32050-0638
904-282-0103

c: The Honorable Ann W. Richards
Governor of Texas
P.O. Box 12428
Austin, Texas 78711

Mr. Mike Wallace

* * * * *

It occurred to me that the Attorney General's office probably heard from a lot of crackpots so I decided to confirm my old relationship with them in the war on drugs.

* * * * *

November 9, 1993

The Honorable Janet Reno
Attorney General of the United States
Department of Justice

Tenth and Constitution Avenue NW
Room 4400
Washington, D.C. 20530

Dear Attorney General:

Following my most recent correspondence, it occurred to me that you undoubtedly get a great deal of mail from those who make outrageous claims with no information regarding their own credibility. In that regard, please find enclosed a letter from the Chairman of the Board of Houston's Drug Free Business Initiative received yesterday. Perhaps it will give you a better feel for my annoyance at the control of Houston's largest newspaper by a cocaine trafficker.

Sincerely,

Roger Hall
P.O. Box 638
Middleburg, Florida 32050-0638
904-282-0103

c: The Honorable Ann W. Richards
   Governor of Texas
   P.O. Box 12428
   Austin, Texas 78711

   Mr. Mike Wallace

*****

December 10, 1993

Mr. William L. Ruzzamenti
Acting Chief

Office of Congressional and Public Affairs
Drug Enforcement Administration
U.S. Department of Justice
Washington, D.C. 20537

Dear Mr. Ruzzamenti:

Thank you for your letter of December 7, 1993, and I look forward to the involvement of DEA in this matter. The copy of this letter will serve as my last direct correspondence to Attorney General Reno, but it is extremely important to me that she know how much I appreciate her finding the time to request the assistance of your organization, especially given the obvious constraints on her time and attention.

Please allow me to interject a few comments that may clarify your personal understanding of this complaint to date. In pursuing a civil action for libel, I learned of prior criminal behavior on the part of a prominent Houstonian. By deposition of the author of the article that prompted the suit, he used the front page of the largest newspaper in Texas as his personal tool in trying cases. The allegation of this type behavior is supported by the enclosed recent article from Texas Monthly magazine. The allegation of criminal activity is based upon the personal involvement and eyewitness knowledge of Mr. Bob Goldstein in a case pursued by the DEA. Bob went to prison in 1985 for Cobra via refusing to cooperate with the DEA in an effort to confirm Cobra's acceptance of large quantities of cash he knew to be drug money as compensation. Bob has now been a productive and useful member of the Houston business community for many years, and remained completely silent about the matter until he saw the devastation of my career and life resulting from the manipulation of the *Houston Chronicle* by Cobra. The position of Mr. Goldstein, and myself for that matter, is that men of criminal nature really should not be in a position of substantial political influence and media control.

I am somewhat concerned about your reference to "appropriate DEA elements" in that Mr. Ruben Monzon, Special Agent In Charge of your Houston office, was informed of this matter by me in the enclosed June 9, 1993 letter. A small collection of documents related to my interaction with DEA is enclosed for your review, and I would have at least expected a phone call or note from the Houston office. To date, nothing has been said, and I received word from a reliable source inside the Department of Justice that Mr. Monzon felt that this issue was politically "messy," and therefore reluctant to become involved. Many evenings of watching interviews with Attorney General Reno on C-SPAN and CNN convinced me that she was sincerely more interested in right and wrong than politics, leading to my pursuit of her attention. In summary, I believe Ruben Monzon to be a completely honest, committed member of law enforcement, but fear that he may honestly be too close to the flame in this case. Support for this position is also provided in the <u>Texas Monthly</u> article, in that Cobra's strong political contacts have become a part of his overt marketing program. Additional concern in this area results from my phone conversation with Bob Goldstein immediately before beginning this correspondence. Several months ago he met with the agent from DEA that sent him to prison (they are now friends), and shared specific names, dates, written records, and other materials regarding these allegations. He has had no response of any kind as of this morning. Should it prove to be the case that the Houston office is proceeding quietly with assimilation of information, I want to apologize in advance for raising these issues. If not, I would like for you to understand that they probably failed to do so for reasonable political motivations. I continue to believe that the people in the Houston office of the DEA are a credit to the Department of Justice, and in no way wish to imply that they are anything else.

Thank you again for your attention. This process has been long, frustrating, and some tell me potentially dangerous. Much of my energy has come from the ongoing belief that somewhere in government, law enforcement, or the legal system there existed at least one completely ethical human being. Your letter served to ratify my hope that Attorney General Reno is that person.

Sincerely,

Roger D. Hall

c: The Honorable Janet Reno
Attorney General of the United States
Department of Justice
Tenth and Constitution Avenue NW
Room 4400
Washington, D.C. 20530

* * * * *

The following was my original letter to Ruben Monzon that accompanied the above correspondence.

* * * * *

June 9, 1993

Mr. Ruben Monzon
Special Agent-In-Charge   <u>Via Express Mail IB212480917</u>
Drug Enforcement Administration
333 West Loop South
Suite 300
Houston, Texas 77024

Dear Mr. Monzon:

You may remember me as the founder of Houston's Drug Free Business Initiative. We met several times due to the involvement of your organization in our sponsorship. On

September 1, 1991 the *Houston Chronicle* ran a front page banner headline story entitled "A Cult of the Wealthy" that inaccurately portrayed me as a former member of a neo-Nazi, homosexual cult. This untrue article effectively destroyed my career, nearly cost me my life, and resulted in a libel suit now scheduled for trial on October 11, 1993. Discovery in this suit and my own investigation have uncovered information that I feel may be important to the Drug Enforcement Administration.

In her initial deposition the author of the article said under oath that the article was "promoted" by Cobra. Since September 25, 1991, I had prevailed upon my legal counsel at the time (Coachwhip et al.) to pursue information I had obtained relevant to the character of Cobra. Specifically, at the time it became necessary to roll down my real estate company due to the damage created by the article, I had a car lease with River Oaks Chrysler Plymouth. The head of the leasing group was an old friend and acquaintance named Bob Goldstein. While discussing the events surrounding my demise, Mr. Goldstein offered me information about Cobra that he had never shared with anyone except his wife. It seems that Bob Goldstein was indicted by your organization on May 1, 1984 in the Western Judicial District of Texas, and sentenced to three years in prison beginning May 1985 for refusing to share information with you about his eye witness knowledge of Cobra's role in money laundering, cocaine trafficking, and one case of attempted murder. Throughout your investigation he was repeatedly assured by both his legal counsel and Cobra that you would not be able to successfully enforce an obscure statute regarding "misprision of a felony." He clearly did not get good information, and saw his business, family, and life disintegrate upon sentencing. Rather than seek retribution on release, Mr. Goldstein quietly went about rebuilding his life, remarried, and has been an honest and faithful employee of Jack Helfman at River Oaks Chrysler for many years.

For years Bob has remained silent about Cobra. I went to Houston to see Bob and his wife on June 4-5, 1993. He has agreed to share dates, names, places, and intricate details about Cobra's character and role in the above referenced activities in order to help me give the jury a feel for the kind of man the largest newspaper in Texas "did a favor," and inadvertently cost me years of building a life and business in Houston. I would welcome the DEA to be a part of the discovery and documentation process.

Additionally, I have filed a complaint with the State Bar of Texas about my original counsel in this case. The attorney assigned to my case after solicitation by Coachwhip was Mr. Cottonmouth, a former employee of the American Civil Liberties Union legal staff, and a specialist in defamation actions. As you see in the selection of correspondence enclosed, for some time I have felt that Cottonmouth and Coachwhip were, for some reason, attempting to undermine my suit. In particular, I was continually frustrated by their refusal to pursue the relevance of Cobra's primary role in the creation of the article. I have now learned that Cobra and Cottonmouth worked closely together on behalf of the ACLU, and are old friends. In your business, you may understand my concern for Cottonmouth's motivation given the input of Mr. Goldstein.

Please pay particular attention to the letter from Coachwhip's attorney dated June 3, 1993. In response to repeated offers on my part to drop the complaint if they would simply agree to submit to gas chromatography drug testing, they have consistently stalled and made unfounded counterclaims rather than take two hours off to go to a testing lab. Note that he avoids making any claims about Cottonmouth drug use, and demands that I put up $25,000 to $30,000 for a $250.00 drug test. It is not necessary to be any smarter than myself to see this as a shallow ploy to delay or avoid testing until Cottonmouth's hair grows to replace the two year limit of gas chromatography reliability. This tactic is particularly distressing to me now that Cottonmouth is employed by the State of Texas Attorney General's Office as a prosecutor. You really wouldn't think submitting to a drug test would be that much of a problem for a key law enforcement agent of the state, would you?

In short, somewhere along the way I fell into a snake pit, and would really like to have some assistance in dealing with the snakes. Thank you for your consideration.

Sincerely,

Roger D. Hall

c: Ms. Elaine Moore - State Bar of Texas
(w/enclosures) <u>via telefacsimile & Express Mail</u>

       Mr. Joe S. Robago, Sr. - State Bar of Texas
(w/enclosures) <u>via telefacsimile & Express Mail</u>

*****

I had decided to find out if there were any honest people left in America, or if I was just another Cicero observing the final days of his Rome.

*****

A few weeks before the hearing Wayne Paris called me, amazed that the appellate hearing had suddenly been moved to an appellate court operating out of Corpus Christi -- outside the sphere of *Chronicle* influence. The appellate hearing was held on December 6, 1993. Wayne told me that all three judges seemed to pay close attention to both sets of arguments -- and that the *Chronicle* lawyers argued Constitutional privilege rather than verity. They had a big contingent. Wayne was alone because I couldn't justify leaving my family alone -- or the money for a plane ticket.

I asked Wayne how long it would take them to decide. He told me that there was no limit on the length of time an appellate court can take to return a decision. If they were going to slam dunk me as the district court had done it would most likely happen quickly, two or three weeks at most. The easy thing for them to do was to say they found no problem with the lower court decision. The longer they took the more it worked in my favor because it meant they were entertaining our arguments that fact issues were present that should be examined at trial. The longest time he had personally ever known an appellate court to take to respond was eight months.

Today is July 15, 1994. The court has not responded in eight months and eight days.

Wayne ran into Hog-nose at the courthouse in Houston a couple of weeks ago. In dramatically uncharacteristic candor, Hog-nose confided to Wayne that he was extremely concerned about the time the appellate court was taking.

* * * * *

It may not make logical sense to anyone else in the world, but the war was over right then and there. I had won.

* * * * *

Saddled with clinical depression and every other problem

of the last nine chapters I had gotten my opponent -- huge, wealthy, vicious, and backed by the Constitution of the United States -- to show some concern over one ragged man who wanted to clear the record.

I had done every single thing available to me short of physical violence to fight back.

My dad said: "They will probably win, but they damn sure know you came through town."

* * * * *

The story of the war will then end with us lying on the ground looking at the grass and taking some deep breaths. There is no need to walk off the field, take a shower, or even to learn the final score. None of those things matter.

This story, and particularly my and my father's hillbilly theory of warfare should not be judged based upon winning or losing. There is an immense difference in winning when you are wrong but have every advantage -- and losing with a clean conscience knowing that you did every single thing any human being could have done.

* * * * *

A good player in any sport knows when it is time to take himself out of a game. Sometimes you fight so hard for so long that the logic leaves you, and you keep fighting even after the final whistle has blown. Then you become just a pitiful joke serving only to amuse the stragglers leaving the stands.

In the interest of myself and my family I have to go to the sideline.

But in the interest of future generations born in the United States of America I can't help hoping that someone bigger and stronger will come along to play these guys. Someone with a whole team, instead of one guy, needs to beat them so bad that the nation takes notice.

They can be beat. If they know how to be afraid they know how to lose.

The Rockies Bring Me Home

> Children know the grace of God
> Better than most of us.
> They see the world
> The way the morning brings it back to them.
> New and born and fresh and wonderful.
>
> Archibald MacLeish, *JB*

How do you know when you are getting better? From psychological illnesses like depression, I mean.

A good Freudian psychotherapist would not see recovery in a patient until he or she was personally ready for retirement. Clinics seem to generally see recovery right about the time insurance coverage stops. Drug companies would argue that real progress is made immediately before the dosage levels of their medications reach a point capable of creating actionable side effects, i.e., death.

I can give you a much more tangible point for when my recovery really began from the events that shattered my life. It was the day that I was able to walk into the Green Cove Springs Athletic Association and coach a team in the lower division of

Little League.

For over two years my life had been consumed by paranoid fear. Even after the "day of transition" I lived in constant fear of having to relive the days of hiding behind trees at West University elementary school when picking up my children for fear of being recognized. Even though we had met some great people in the Clay county YMCA soccer program, there was no way that I could run the risk of accepting a head coaching position. Any dispute of any kind might lead to a telephone call to Houston and transmission of the virulent misinformation that I was all the things I had never been. My self-imposed special forces training had slowly built a facade of confidence. I had never in my life, for even a moment been a Nazi, a woman hater, or a homosexual. In fact, the only two boys I had ever even kissed were my dad and Jeremy. Better yet, it was the public exposure of those sick bastards that had caused my trouble. Now I was perfectly willing and able to whip anyone's ass who wanted to imply that there was any truth to other renditions of my past.

Additionally, and to her great credit, my side of the story had become public through Jane Wolfe's book *Blood Rich* for Little, Brown. Jane had talked to me in Houston, and she was one of the few people who had been given the opportunity to read the early version of this book's first chapter. Her own exhaustive research had confirmed my story, and although her book rips the throat out of the Wyatt family and the involvement of Doug and his mother in Eternal Values I came out looking pretty good. And guess what? Neither the *Houston Chronicle* or the Wyatt family disputed her version of the story. Pretty strange for the defendants of some ugly allegations on my part to avoid confronting a major book supporting my claims, huh?

The ultimate test of becoming some of my former self was to be able to do what had been one of my favorite things -- coaching youth athletics. It was still unclear as to whether I would ever be able to walk into the middle of a group of kids and begin to teach them again.

Our experiences with soccer and gymnastics in the area had been good. Elyssa had a great time with her classes before they were preempted by her newfound love of horses. Jeremy started on a soccer team that got stomped every time they walked on the field, but thanks to sticking together and two great coaches they won their league in the third season.

It was one of the two soccer coaches who suggested we look into having his son and Jeremy play baseball together. Shelly and I had already ruled out a small association league that we took Jeremy to shortly after moving in. He was fortunate to have had a wonderful man as his coach, but much of the league leadership was comprised of belligerent redneck stock and it showed through every level of play. Our coach and friend lived in Green Cove Springs so we decided to at least go look at the program.

The Saturday for sign up was a beautiful crisp spring morning, and one look at the four playing fields told me a lot. Virtually all the league officials, coaches, and players came from working families. The athletic association most certainly did not have the money to hire caretakers, but the field condition would have been acceptable for a major league playoff game.

We were introduced to the league president and the minor league coordinator. Both worked far in excess of forty hours per week, but came to the complex four nights per week from 5 p.m. to 10 p.m. to oversee activities. The days of use said a lot about the community. There were no weekend games to give families a chance to do something together. There were no Wednesday night games to keep from interfering with church. But mistaking only four play days for lack of interest was definitely a mistake. Baseball was serious business here.

Full of coffee and spring fever I was in a weak position when they told me that the minor league had a serious coaching shortage. My friend from soccer was tied up in a three-month-long class at church with his wife and had three boys involved in a variety of activities. As president of a successful small oil company he was strapped for time and could only commit to serving as assistant. Before I knew what happened, it was done. I was head coach of the Green Cove Springs Rockies.

The season is nearly over at the time this chapter is being written, and it would take another book to cover all the things that have transpired. We were just like the real Rockies --

happy, colorful, loved by our fans, and absolutely trampled by everyone we played in the beginning. But by the end of the season we were nobody's doormat anymore. My twelve-year-old black kid that no one else would take in the draft after tryouts could not hit a barn door with a tennis racket when the season started. By the end of the season other teams would back their outfielders up against the fence every time he came to the plate. My other black kid (I had 66 2/3% of the black kids in the league) did not even have baseball as a concept when we began. He got the game ball last week for going three for three with a double, two singles, and three RBIs. The stories go on and the point is the same. Everyone grew, especially me.

Theoretically all minor league teams should have had the same amount of talent. In reality the new guy on the block ends up with the kids no one else wants, especially with regard to the eight-year-olds who do not go to tryouts. I struck back with capitalism. Even though my income was nothing like the past my wife made a lot of money by area standards, and she was foolish enough to allow me to retain a Visa card. In an area where three dollars for a new little league ball was not a trivial expense, and twenty-five dollars for a real major league Colorado Rockies hat was outrageous, we had more giveaways than a Chinese restaurant owned by a camera manufacturer. All players got a ball when they got their first hit. Player or players (depending on whether I had any money) of the month got a hat. Those hitting home runs got a hat. Player of the game, even when we lost by fifteen runs, got a game ball. Most days we had two game balls -- one for the real player of the game and one for someone I knew was having a bad time for one reason or another.

We got trounced eleven games out of twelve, having won one against the second-worst team in the league to the unimaginable delight of our loyal parents and fans. Game thirteen was against a team that had beaten us twice, coached by a nice but extremely competitive man with a top management job in the county administration. He had two sons on the team, one of whom was in my daughter's fourth-grade class. The day of the game his son told my daughter that it was their day off because they were playing the Rockies. Not only did he publicly announce that we were the worst team in the league, but he was actually laughing at us. Harboring some doubt about the degree of validity coming from a fourth grader having her first run-in with hormones, I blew it off until we got to the field for warm-up. The opponents were trickling in and laughing at my guys as they took batting practice. You can laugh at me. You can blame the record on me. Hell, you can paste my picture on the front page of the largest newspaper in Texas and tell the world all sorts of lies about me. But you can't laugh at my team.

The Rockies had made steady improvement all season. Each player had made huge individual strides in becoming a real baseball player and had loads of fun making them. But we were not ready for this team and would not be for another year.

Not once during the season had I said a single word about winning. But before the first inning began, I took the Rockies to the dugout and told them about my daughter's day in class. They told me about things the other team had said during pregame practice. We agreed that we wanted to win. The next two hours were one of the highlights of my life.

Our outfielders were catching fly balls instead of shielding their faces with gloves. Our worst hitters were beating out infield singles by diving into the bag at first base. We got an unassisted double play from Jeremy who caught a fly ball near the pitcher's mound and then ran down a runner hung up between first base and second base.

Before I knew what happened it was the middle of the sixth with the other team coming to bat for the last time and us leading 15-10. There was a five run per inning cap so we could not possibly lose. It made the '69 Mets a mere footnote in baseball history by comparison.

They had two runs in with runners on first and second. There were two outs. Their best hitter took a fifty-mile-an-hour fastball from the pitching machine and slammed it down the third base line straight at one of my two best fielders. All he had to do was step on the bag to seal the greatest victory in modern sports history. The ball went directly between his legs untouched, past my left fielder, and all the way to the fence. We were playing on one of the larger fields and by the time my big kid from left center got to the ball the hitter was trotting into home with an inside-the-park home run.

We tied.

The other coach was absolutely shell-shocked as we lined up to walk across and shake hands with all the opposing players. We had a strict rule against saying anything negative to anyone, whether they be on our team or another. My guys were ecstatic. His were somber.

"You've got them looking good."

"Thanks. We're trying."

I told my assistant coach, now a close friend, that the tie was God's way of having Karma teach us all a lesson. They learned humility, and I learned not to want to win so much.

It was next to impossible to go to sleep that night, and while staring at the ceiling fan I realized that for the first time in two years I had really been in Green Cove Springs, Florida. Not up in my head thinking about my war with the Hearst corporation or money or lost clients or lawyers. I had really been at a Little League game. It was a crack in the wall that let a trickle of water through. In the months that followed the trickle became a roaring torrent of change. Finally it became a deep and slow moving river.

All the days from the beginning of the problem started and ended with the 23rd Psalm. He had finally gotten me to lie down in the green pastures and led me beside the still waters. He had restored my soul.

The hate was gone. The martial arts and military training

continued but became a science rather than a paranoid obsession. Houston finally became a part of my past.

The Rockies reflected all the problems of society -- poverty, parents with drug and alcohol problems, naive adherence to religious dogma, divorce...

The Rockies reflected all the good of society -- healthy and loved children, doting parents, good manners, concern for others...

But first and foremost the Rockies were a pure expression of the best part of the human race -- children. Children who were honest, eager to learn, and genuinely appreciative of the most simple kindness or compliment.

For my fortieth birthday the Rockies gave me an alligator head because they knew I liked to hunt reptiles. At the end of the season party they gave me a baseball autographed by each of them, a real Colorado Rockies shirt with each of their names and numbers printed on the back, and a key chain engraved with "Coach Hall" on the front and "You Made A Difference - Rockies 94" on the back. There was no way to explain it to them, but they had also given me back a part of myself that I had thought was gone forever.

* * * * *

There are things in this book that the thirteen Rockies never need to know. There are uses of language and recounts of events that are not for small eyes. But someone has to try to fix the greatest country in the history of mankind in the spots where it is broken so the Rockies can someday watch their grandchildren catch fire for one evening of baseball magic.

The Rockies brought me home to a place I had never been before.

I was finally okay.

Hunting Snakes In Peace

"The youth gets together his materials to build a bridge to the moon, or, perchance, a palace or temple on the earth, and, at length, the middle-aged man concludes to build a woodshed with them."

Henry David Thoreau, <u>Journal - July 14, 1852</u>

I woke up around five this morning, put on some coffee, and headed straight for the garage refrigerator. Our newest family member, a black lab/pit bull mix who had not so long ago been only a few minutes away from euthanasia, headed me off for a bit of ear scratching and chit chat. When we met at the pound he had been so overwhelmed by genetically predisposed mange that all the hair was gone from his head and neck. Stuffed in a cage with five larger puppies he had been covered in excrement. He charged the front of the cage when he saw me, stuck both front paws through the wire, and started clawing the air. Not needing any more pets but refusing to succumb to good judgment I bent over for a closer look. Five hundred dollars in vet bills later he is beginning to look pretty good. There goes the summer vacation. Shelly took my Visa card away too.

We named him "Little Dog" as kind of a backhanded shot at the minority opinion held by some locals about animals, i.e., "it's just a damned old dog -- ya orta just shoot the sumbitch." Living here is becoming more comfortable every day, but there are some who desperately need to read (or have read to them) my short story "Revenge of the White Tail" about a man who dons a deerskin and a catcher's mask equipped with antlers to do a bit of his own hunting.

I have met some of the finest people in my life here, and some of the most disgusting redneck trash. But then that's true of just about everywhere, isn't it?

Back to the dog. Little Dog is quickly proving himself to be the smartest dog I have ever known. And what I like best about him is that he only has two gears. With the neighborhood children he is all Black Lab -- swimming, chasing sticks, climbing up into a lawn chair for his afternoon nap. With strangers, and especially the poor guy from UPS, he is all pit bull.

Little Dog and his two adopted siblings, Pebbles the Weimeraner and Dizzy the Black Lab, couldn't understand why I didn't immediately raise the garage door for our morning ritual of sitting for dog biscuit communion and confession of overnight sins -- cat treeing, flower bed digging, shoe chewing, etc.

They were locked outside this morning because I had work to do. Opening the storage refrigerator I removed a ten gallon plastic bucket containing seven or so gallons of diamondback rattlesnake. Figuring that he was mellow enough from his night of chilling to head into the formaldehyde without protest I just dumped him on the cement floor and reached for one of the Lipton sun tea jars that are used to hold really attractive or rare specimens.

While dumping the snake on the warm floor I was struck by the size of his head. He was only about five feet long, which was not enormous by rattlesnake standards, but his triangular head was at least three inches wide. This guy was custom designed for killing things.

Before I could get the jar open there came an all too familiar rattling sound behind me. Whether the refrigerator temperature was set too high or he was just a tough customer was irrelevant at the moment -- all I could think about was having on shorts and sandals. I turned to see him two feet away, pulling his neck back into the center of his body as he assumed a coiled position.

After jumping about five feet up and two feet back I grabbed my homemade snake stick and managed to get the loop around his neck just as he became fully wound. Holding the suddenly wide awake rattler in one hand my search was on for some heavy gloves with the other. After finding a pair of scuba diving gloves on a nearby shelf the issue became whether to bravely choke the unruly guest to death or to stuff him in something for later. Choking cottonmouths had for a time been the great source of release for my internalized rage -- it was a whole lot cheaper than psychotherapy and infinitely less time consuming.

But of all the snakes I had seen this guy was easily the most vicious. Choosing discretion over valor he went into a yellow canvas bag for some mood altering freezer time. In two hours his attitude was much improved, and he is now one of the most striking specimens in my preserved collection.

* * * * *

Venomous snakes are all over the place. They have tiny brains, big fangs, and are hard to kill. No matter how you treat them they will still be venomous, aggressive, and predatory.

The same goes for some humans. Most are harmless and are only trying to get by. For the most part they engage in symbiotic behavior. They are the ones that need the protection of laws in a civilized land. Others will be dangerous no matter how hard you may try to change them.

There is a line I used to use with my liberal friends when defending my support of George Bush: "If at twenty you are not a liberal you have no heart. If at forty you are not a conservative you have no brain." It works on libel law and snakes as well.

I've learned that I have to deal with people the way they deal with me. If I am cruel or unfair to the good it will come back to me in a larger dose. If I try to appease the evil they become larger, more lethal forms of evil. Pretending that one can make something good of a rattlesnake or cottonmouth is self-delusion.

I have also learned that issues are almost always more complex than they seem. For example, I spent two years of my free time in Houston generating money and support for George Bush the first time he ran for president. He had become my choice after I found a copy of an old autobiography titled *George Bush* at the downtown Houston public library. It was published many years before *Looking Forward* came out as a part of the campaign, and it stands out as one of the best short descriptions of character I have ever read. Although the familiar stories of bravery in battle and success in virtually every endeavor were impressive, the most important section of the book dealt with how he and Mrs. Bush coped with the death of their own child. Robin's death from leukemia changed the future president's attitude about what he wanted to accomplish in life and led to pursuit of a career in public service rather than in business. His mother had taught him humility and his daughter had taught him the value of a single human life. He also had the backing of one of the finest women in American history. George Bush was the perfect man to be president.

As much as I admired George Bush and wished we had all been fortunate enough to have had mothers like Barbara Bush, it became necessary for me to vote for Bill Clinton in 1992. Bush's administration had failed to fulfill its promises regarding my most important personal issue -- child care for the poor in pursuit of education or any other means of escaping poverty. President Bush seemed to be absolutely hamstrung when it came to making major decisions on this or any other domestic issue. In retrospect, much of his image problem was the direct result of media manipulation. The liberal press had decided that it was time for someone more interesting to become the target of their ongoing news generation. Still President Bush seemed to me to owe too many favors to too many people, and genuinely wanted to make everyone happy. These two realities merged to create a stalemate on many critical issues. But what a thing to say about the President of the United States! You can only be President if you are callous and vicious enough to betray your old friends and survive the media. Especially survive the media.

In short, George Bush was too good and nice a man to be the President of the United States. He had no extramarital affairs or shaky real estate deals to supplement the more mundane daily issues of nuclear threats posed by Asian madmen or collapse of the world economy.

President Clinton may still surprise us all. He really is the Eveready Rabbit -- he just keeps going and going and . . . . He has aged visibly in the first two years, but he shows signs of being enough of a warrior to survive the continual onslaught of second guessing and harassment by the media. And thank God for pinnacle products of our culture like Tonya Harding and O.J. Simpson. At least for a while the reptiles of the press have had other warm meat to swallow whole without focusing only on the President of the United States. But once again, if Bill Clinton fails it will be primarily because he was not mean enough.

Do we as a nation really want to continue to make callousness and viciousness required character traits for our leaders? Are those of you sitting on the Supreme Court really proud of the evolution of libel law that has played a great role in converting me from a fiscally conservative, socially liberal successful businessman into a snake strangling recluse who spends thirty minutes a day driving his fingers into a bucket of stainless steel ball bearings in preparation for ripping the trachea and esophagus from a hired killer?

Even if my belief proves to be trauma-related paranoia that criminals like Cobra have gained such a high level of control in America that the real threat to my family may not be a single professional assassin but instead a murderous onslaught by law enforcement officials acting at the orders of Cobra's powerful friends -- was the trauma that led to the insanity really necessary? What exactly was it that I did that made me deserving of the last three years? How did a group of self-righteous reporters come to have more rights than me in a country that was founded on the belief that we were all equal under the law? Would the personal lives and professional accomplishments of those who tell us what to think really stand up well if the same level of scrutiny were applied to them that they apply to the rest of us?

And lest you too easily accept the paranoia option, remember that even though David Koresh was clearly an evil man in need of restraint a thousand opportunities to seize him individually while jogging or going to bars around Waco were passed by in favor of a Gestapo-style assault that ultimately resulted in the muffled screams of innocent children as they burned to death while the cameras rolled. The blood of those children can never be washed from the hands of this nation, and neither can the memory of all the journalists who reported and denounced the carnage with a twinkle in their eye and reports of high ratings on their desks.

* * * * *

For both public and private persons the law of libel must once again be allowed to protect our rights. The respectable members of the press will not cause harm because it is not their nature to cause harm. The rattlers and cottonmouths of the media will not change on their own. They need freezer time in the form of actual and punitive damages handed out by a court system that has been restored its ability to protect the rights of an individual.

* * * * *

What will become of me? I have no clue -- and that is one

of the reasons why it was important to write this section prior to any decision by the appellate court on reversing or upholding the summary judgment in my case against Hearst.

My wife always knows what I am thinking, usually as I am thinking it and sometimes before. The reality is that in order to be happy I have to be busy doing something productive. Being financially dependent on her is an impossible condition for me to tolerate, and her repeated line about my supporting her for nineteen years which suggests that she owes me nineteen might work for some -- but not with one who was raised like I was.

There was a time when I told my friend Congressman Jack Fields that I wanted to some day be secretary of state in order to play a role in what then President Bush called the "New World Order." Now I just want to get myself together enough to get a job.

I feel I was the best commercial real estate broker in America. Not the highest income broker -- having the integrity to be the best demands forfeiture of any chance to make the most money. The snakes in that pit have already proven that they will not give me time to grab the snake stick if I try to get back in, so I will be content with the peaceful placement of my name in a Brokerage Hall of Fame of my own creation.

My wife wanted me to go to law school for a while. For some reason she thought that my untutored first try score in the 96th percentile on the Law School Admission Test, innate warrior tendencies, and compassion for the downtrodden would be a valuable combination. The University of Florida School of Law is only a ninety-minute drive from my home, and for a while specializing in legal malpractice did seem to hold promise as a career where I could make money and have fun too.

But if I took out fifty sleazy lawyers in the next twenty years there would be fifty-one more to take their places. They seem to be multiplying faster than the cottonmouths. And I am very weary of days spent pursuing negativity.

My personal choice at present is to sit here and document my observations on the continued decline of what has been for more than two hundred twenty years the greatest country in the history of mankind. The selfishness and shallowness that has propagated disintegration of the family, the AIDS epidemic, virtual reality in lieu of reality, and sound bytes of poison rather than symphonies of truth will drive this nation to its knees if left unchecked.

My theory on curbing the scourge of drug abuse in this country has gained enough credibility to have the federal government pump millions of dollars into the program I went door to door in Houston to create. But there is not a great deal left of the bright-eyed, bushy-tailed dreamer who set out to cure the world's drug problem. Neither is there is any real hope that my suggestions on remedy of the credibility crisis of our media in Chapter Twelve will ever be read, much less implemented by anyone who can affect change. There is then perhaps only the role of a detached and increasingly disinterested historian.

So I guess I am going to be a writer. It will also be necessary to get a manual labor day job to avoid the depression resulting from feelings of parasitism.

* * * * *

At least three things need to be said to make this work honest before closing to Chapter Twelve and my suggestions for reform of libel law.

The first is that there were plenty of ugly things the *Houston Chronicle* could have said about me that would have been true and therefore not defamatory. For example, I do not drink or take illegal drugs -- nor did I during the period of recruitment by Doug Wyatt and Eternal Values. But there were plenty of times in my younger years when those comments would have been true. The truth is that my commitment to building a successful anti-drug program was the direct result of experience with what I believe to be the insidious threat and metaphysical evil of substance abuse.

Second, I have never hated any people on the basis of race, creed, color, sex, or natural origin. But for most of the past three years I have harbored a very real and very pathological group hatred of lawyers and reporters. It is no more justifiable in the light of day than hatred of any other group. It was wrong to have ever been filled with hate, I am sorry for it, and sincerely believe that it is behind me. Still I wish to apologize to any member of either of those professions for my enmity.

Finally, a number of good things have resulted from the changes in my life. My children are better for having the opportunity to grow up in Clay County, Florida. It is a place where law and order, family orientation, and concern for others are alive and well. My life is better for having the opportunity to see what a group of unselfish physicians can do for economically disadvantaged children -- and to know that in a small way I was able to contribute to the cause by helping one of their best realize her potential.

I am a lucky man for having the opportunity to spend so much time with my own children. When they were small much of our interaction was as superficial as handing over an airport gift shop toy in the morning before running off in pursuit of money and ego again. They are my best friends as well as my children, and seeing them grow and learn on a minute by minute basis is a luxury of the highest order.

I never expected to play football and front a blast furnace to get through college, fight to the top of a lucrative profession, garner praise as an up-and-coming star in American business and public service -- only to end up spending so much time cooking, cleaning house, doing laundry, and serving as a taxi driver for children. But then I never would have known what a pleasure and honor it was to do those things for those whom you love -- or how valuable a service it is that comes from so many who receive so little credit. And "He Thinks He'll Keep Her" by Mary Chapin-Carpenter would have never assumed a position in my mind alongside "Give Peace A Chance" as one of the premier protest songs of all time.

So the truth is that I was never all good and the result of the damage has not been all bad. The knowledge that I will never be wealthy in a material sense seems to be less important to me every day.

If I can take the final steps to get beyond the sadness and depression that still lurk in the shadows, I will be a better human being for the experience.

The Rockies brought me down out of my own head to see that this is a wonderful place with many wonderful people. Recently it seems that there may be a remedy for the lingering dark episodes that would not have ever been available in the city. There are nine hundred undeveloped acres next to my home. In the beginning the land served only as a place to hunt snakes. These days when the depression hits I just go for long walks into the forest. On a walk not long ago it seemed that there was someone watching me -- an absolute knowledge of some presence, but no sign of life other than mosquitos and moths. After several minutes of looking around on ground level I finally looked up. Less than twenty yards away sat a huge owl on the branch of a tree. We stared at each other for over an hour and seemed to be in agreement that although the focus of our respective attention might be odd it was harmless. Finally I walked away as he was still watching -- having completely forgotten what it was that had so upset me before the walk.

My snake hunting expeditions have evolved into a personal study of the vanishing grandeur that is north Florida. Snakes often slither away unmolested these days as I am preoccupied with a new wildflower in bloom or a tiny change in the course of a stream resulting from a recent rain. My children have found magic buried in the gravel runs of Black Creek. Magic in the form of arrowheads and artifacts left by the Seminoles in the days before reservations, barbed-wire fences, and tabloid newspapers.

There is also magic in the relief of internal turmoil by something as simple as a walk in the forest.

* * * * *

Just like the introduction said, this book had to be written. No one has to read it, but it had to be written.

Today is July 8, 1994. I am exactly forty years and two months old. John Lennon was exactly forty years and two months old when his life ended. He left more positive change and hope for change than any other man in my lifetime. In the spirit of Jesus Christ, Mahatma Ghandi, and Martin Luther King he accomplished his goals through peaceful protest rather than violence. He changed the world for the better and he changed music forever. He did it all in forty years and two months.

I made enough money to buy Miami (but I pissed it away so fast. . . .Thank you, Mr. Buffett), won lots of awards, and chased lots of dreams in my first forty years and two months. But this book is the first material thing of my own creation that has much value to me. There are no more John Lennons, but we all have an obligation to do what we can to make the world a better place. This book was all that I could do. Under the circumstances it was the best that I could do.

I can't afford to get the book printed yet, but someday I will. I certainly can't make any member of the Supreme Court read it, but I can and will put it in the mail.

It was very important to me to get this chapter done today before getting any older.

Suggestions to the High Court

"The man who never looks into a newspaper is better informed than he who reads them; inasmuch as he who knows nothing is nearer to truth than he whose mind is filled with falsehood and errors."

Thomas Jefferson, letter to John Norvell, 1807

"Laws and institutions must go hand in hand with the progress of the human mind."

Thomas Jefferson, letter to Samuel Kercheval, 1816

"We have plenty of lawyers down here at the courthouse -- what we need are some people with common sense."

Anonymous Houston Public Defender to Potential Jurors, 1992

There are four books that occupy permanent positions on my desk -- the *NIV Study Bible*, the *Bhagavad Gita*, *Yogas and Other Works* by Swami Vivekananda, and *The Jefferson Bible*. Of those, Mr. Jefferson's struggle to make sense of Christianity is by far the most readable.

Thomas Jefferson had the ability to condense vast amounts of information to a few succinct elements. In tribute to his genius and concision I will offer seven brief suggestions for advancement and humanization of libel law.

Before turning to the thoughts on improvement please allow me to reiterate a fundamental observation of the introduction:

> I do not harbor any resentment or hatred of the press. To the contrary each of my days is filled with reading -- often the output of the media. There are some incredibly gifted and ethical journalists in each branch of media. Different parts of *Freedom From The Press* were written at different times. Some of those times were filled with depression, resentment, and hatred. Please try to overlook the emotion of those periods should you choose to proceed, and remember that by the time you reach my specific suggestions to you in Chapter Twelve the mood will be that of this introduction.

I would like to think that the promise has been kept. Looking back at the pages before there is considerably more hate and paranoia than I would have wished. There is nothing that can be done about that, but as this final chapter in the three lost years of my life begins my thoughts turn to Walter Cronkite. As a small child I remember hearing "And that's the way it is" and feeling as if my grandfather had spoken the words. If Walter Cronkite said it -- it had to be true.

There are no more Walter Cronkites, but I sense the same

integrity and believability in segments done by Mike Wallace or Ed Bradley on 60 Minutes. Even if they did broadcast a segment that was false or misleading I would want to believe it was an honest mistake rather than an attempt at sensationalistic ratings generation. In the same vein I would be severely disheartened to think that Diane Sawyer would ever make a personal decision to advance her personal success at the cost of the truth. She just strikes me as someone you would have liked to have had as a friend. And even though Dan Rather attacked Vice President Bush at a time when I was fighting desperately to raise money for him in the economic depression of Texas in the 1980s I believe that Mr. Rather is a man of great integrity when taken as a whole. On another tangent of a virtually infinite spectrum Rush Limbaugh might, on the rare occasion, bend the facts to fit his theories, but he is clearly a man of great integrity and conviction. There are many others that do a tremendous job of bringing the light of knowledge into our lives.

My point is that I really have escaped the trap of virulent hatred for the media. There are many members of the profession who have lived their lives in such a way as to create lasting value for society far beyond my own original dreams and goals. To hate or distrust any group of human beings based upon a profession would make me guilty of the same sins as the neo-Nazis whose exposure led to my destruction.

Regarding suppression of speech or prior licensing all I can tell you is that my life is better for having had the opportunity to read the diverse works of Hunter Thompson, P.J. O'Rourke, George Will, and Richard Nixon. The ability to express differing and even radical views is more important today than ever before. Suppression of the truth would ultimately be lethal to any free society. My suggestions are ones of correction rather than suppression. My hope is that they emphasize the truth while protecting the fundamental freedom of the media.

In the attempt to stay one step ahead of the competition, all sources of news will inevitably make mistakes by virtue of haste. We expect the trash decorating the racks of the check-out area of grocery stores to be filled with lies and half truths, but even the most venerable and responsible of media institutions have come to regularly cause some harm to innocent people as an unfortunate but nonetheless inescapable byproduct of their activities.

* * * * *

How then would a man who has seen his life destroyed and literally been left for dead by the powerful Hearst Corporation and its respected counsel propose to correct a system spinning out of control?

Here are my seven recommendations:

Consider Thomas Jefferson's comment on the interrelationship of law with the progress of the human mind when considering First Amendment issues.

President John Kennedy once began his address to a group of Nobel laureates having dinner at the White House by noting that it was the greatest assemblage of talent and intelligence gathered in the room since Thomas Jefferson had dined alone.

If Mr. Jefferson were to return briefly to review his country how do you suppose he would he would personally rate the evolution of First Amendment law?

Did he and his cohorts really intend to create a system that would come to allow open lies, misleading use of facts, trials in the "court of public opinion," and glorification of human slaughter as the primary means of conflict resolution?

After an evening of watching prime time television and late night movies while flipping through the pages of *Hustler*, *The National Enquirer*, and *Soldier of Fortune* would Mr. Jefferson be proud of the progress of our minds?

Is there any chance that I might garner Mr. Jefferson's support for my argument that doing a favor for a cocaine trafficker and inadvertently destroying my reputation is not Constitutionally protected behavior for the largest newspaper in Texas?

Rather than carry the point to absurdity let me implore you to take your heads up from the never-ending reams of paper for a moment to look around and compare where we started out to go with where we are.

Remove any distinction between private and public figures in the law of defamation.

As a private figure who has been through the trenches of libel law I can only imagine how much worse it is to be a public figure.

John F. Kennedy, Jr. recently said in a television interview that if his father were alive today he would probably not enter politics because of the constant media intrusion into the private lives of public figures.

Professor Lucas Powe of the University of Texas School of Law noted in *The Fourth Estate and the Constitution: Freedom of the Press in America* that we have created a system where only the most cold and brazen of people can withstand the onslaught of media abuse and defamation that accompanies public service. I sincerely believe that, if left unchecked, this reality of public life will in itself lead to the downfall of this nation.

Avoid the possibility of defamation by allowing the subjects of potentially damaging material an opportunity to review the materials referring to them.

My life would have been much better today if it had been possible for me to call the manager of the *Chronicle* (and father of a great little boy on my tee-ball team) to request that his reporter allow me to review the article prior to publication. Two words in the cutline of one picture could have been changed, and this book would never have needed to be written. The two words would not have changed their story. They would have dramatically changed my life. The press needs to get over its resistance to allowing the subjects access to information. As you will see in a moment there will still be no barriers to printing the truth in any form, but the truth is more likely to be known by someone involved with an issue or event for twenty years than by one involved for twenty minutes.

A fair and realistic opportunity to review materials in final form should be an absolute defense for the media in the event of even unforeseen damage. In essence: "You are a reasonable man. You read it. You thought it was okay. We are not liable."

In the event of harm, temporally appropriate retraction or correction of materials in a fashion as identical to the damaging transmission as reasonably possible should be an absolute defense for the media.

If Richard Nixon had taken the same approach to Watergate that Lee Iacocca took to the Chrysler odometer rollback fiasco he might have had a lot less trouble in the later years of his life.

What's wrong with admitting that we screwed up?

In the early 1980s a book titled *Service America* reported that 95% of Americans would do business again with someone who made a mistake, promptly admitted it, and took steps toward rectification. A sincere apology and correction made customers much more likely to do business with those who had repaired unintentional damage than their competitors in the marketplace who had no history with the customer.

Professor Powe reports that the most prevalent media reaction to individual requests for remedy as "Fuck you -- you're full of shit."[6] This attitude is not worthy of a group empowered by the First Amendment to the Constitution of the United States.

On the other side of the issue I am not sure that plaintiffs (at least myself) are much better when it comes to avoidance of conflict. Instead of contacting the source of the damage and at least requesting a correction my reaction was to go to lawyers who would sue them. My experience, aided by hindsight, is that civil litigation in this country has become a sad joke. Attorneys and experienced combatants in the system consistently told me that going to the courthouse these days is at best a "crapshoot." The brother of my surgeon friend from chapter one (former associate of Miami's most prestigious law firm) told me that for a while rich people and wealthy companies liked the system because they could spend their way to victory in almost any dispute. He went on to say that as of March 1993 the system was so screwed up that even rich people and wealthy companies hated it, therefore causing billing problems for his firm.

Even if you do not agree that the wheels have come off the system you may agree that we sue each other too often in this country. Given your docket I feel pretty comfortable about

---

[6]Powe, Lucas A. The Fourth Estate and the Constitution: Freedom of the Press in America. University of California Press (1991), p. 116.

agreement on this one, and I would like to suggest that we keep defamation resolution out of the court system if possible.

Those injured by the media, whether they be public or private figures, should have a right to approach the injuring party on a formal basis outside the legal system to request repair of the damage. There should be presentation of a written explanation detailing what portion of the information transmitted was wrong, the extent of damage or potential damage, and supporting evidence for the claim or claims.

Should the media agree that they made a mistake, prompt retraction or correction would be an absolute defense against further legal action. If the media is going to choke on this method of conflict avoidance it will probably be on the requirement that the retraction or correction be "in a fashion as identical to the damaging transmission as reasonably possible." Cutting my throat on the front page of a holiday Sunday edition and expecting to retract in a small paragraph on page twelve of Thursday's paper is not a solution. This is a call for "a printed eye for a printed eye, and a printed tooth for a printed tooth." Anything less would be unfair and of less than no value.

If we could hope for a higher standard of human behavior in America for a moment perhaps we could entertain the notion that organizations like Hearst might raise fixing their mistakes to an art form. Would it really be so terrible to pick up the paper every day and see four of five "What we should have said. . ." stories? I don't think so. It might even make us comfortable that the information we get is either true, or will be soon.

Should step four fail to provide mutually acceptable remedy, the opposing parties would be required to attempt mediation prior to litigation.

Litigation is psychologically devastating for defamation plaintiffs, expensive for defendants, and in its present state of no value in preserving the visionary goals of the First Amendment.

So send me to pick a mediator. Send Hearst to pick one. Then require the two mediators to pick a mutually acceptable third mediator to serve as a tie breaker. Make us share the costs to avoid frivolous disputes. Make the plaintiff responsible for the fees and costs of the media defendant if the claim is found to be frivolous and the media defendant liable for fees, costs, and <u>actual</u> damages only in the event they are found to be in the wrong and guilty of denying the wrong in the face of evidence.

If mediation fails send the combatants to court. Make the losing party responsible for all fees and costs of the prevailing party. Keep the burden of proof for the falsity of the publication or transmission on the plaintiff. But for God's sake make it a fair fight.

This is neither the time nor the place to take up tort reform, but should everything else fail we need to assume that litigation in its current condition is still better than violence.

If a plaintiff did something onerous and was discovered, refuses to admit it, then makes his adversary run up a lot of costs defending the reporting of truth they deserve to inherit a substantial financial burden.

If the media defendants are presented with the truth and choose to disregard it make them subject to the same potential penalties as other personal injury defendants. My actual damages are real. Given the behavior of the defendant I feel that twelve of my peers might agree that a message should have been sent in the form of punitive damages. Why, after the opportunities afforded in steps one through three to avoid all monetary risk should the defendant be further shielded? We need to remember that there will always be some segment of any profession that cares for nothing but money. Taking it away will be the only way to get their attention.

Never lose sight of the rights of one human being.

I have been betrayed by the Supreme Court of the United States of America. I have been denied my constitutionally protected right to life, liberty, and the pursuit of happiness. I have been unfairly treated as a criminal without due process or a speedy trial. The laws of the land have served to protect a true criminal in his manipulation of a major source of information for personal gain.

There is no information available to make me believe that the First Amendment to the Constitution was intended to deny me the rights that have been stripped away by the *New*

York Times v. Sullivan decision and subsequent interpretation.

I am only one citizen of the United States of America. It is up to you to decide if my rights are important or not.

* * * * *

There have been a number of proposals to reform libel law over the past few years. An excellent review of the essential components of most of them exists in Chapters 2-9 of *Reforming Libel Law* (edited by John Soloski and Randall P. Bezanson; Guilford Press, 1992). No doubt the physicians will continue to debate as the patients die on the tables, citing reams of evidence and volumes of case law in support of some particular avenue of reform that best suits their legal specialty or personal needs. The defense attorneys will fight like mad to maintain the status quo for the simple and arguably sensible reasons verbalized by Robert Sack, himself a media defense specialist:

> "Yes, Virginia, if you are a media defense attorney, there is a Santa Claus; it's your client, which unintentionally, but surely, harms some of the people it writes about."[7]

The defense attorneys and their wealthy clients will redouble their efforts to avoid change because of the current imbalance of power and the odds of any plaintiff winning under

---

[7] Powe, Lucas A., Jr., <u>The Fourth Estate and the Constitution: Freedom of the Press in America</u>, University of California Press, 1991.

the current system. Again counting on the eloquence of Mr. Sack to help make my point:

> "The few plaintiffs who succeed resemble the remnants of an army platoon caught in an enemy crossfire. Their awards stand witness to their good luck, not to their virtue, their skill or the justice of their cause."[8]

As a group the libel plaintiffs in America who have been injured by transmission of false information have considerably less chance of survival than the proverbial snowball in Hell. The vast majority of libel claims are settled by summary judgment in favor of the defendant -- usually with the justification of Constitutional privilege. But even then 60% of summary judgments (including mine) are appealed. We may be out of money, beaten down, and even clinically ill as a result of the libel but still we fight on. It is a strange and illogical war that we wage -- but for all the reasons I have tried to share in this work we have no other option. And throughout our illogical and hopeless war the defense attorney's meter runs while their clients bask in the knowledge that the *New York Times v. Sullivan* decision makes them practically omnipotent.

If you continue to allow denial of the individual rights of libel plaintiffs within the system you will eventually force them to seek retribution outside the system. There was a brief period of time after coming to grips with the slender margin that

---

[8]Ibid.

separated my life from death when I daydreamed of taking a Tec-9 pistol with a thirty-shot clip into Houston and seeking my own justice. It was fear of the consequences for my wife and children that prevented another morbid footnote in American history, not fear of my own demise or respect for the corrupt and unfair system that had repeatedly kicked me down its marble steps. Although at this later date I am ashamed of even the fleeting thought of violence not necessary for self defense, I feel that the High Court may consider shouldering a bit of the blame and remorse. It would never have happened if the Court of 1964 had not set in motion a series of events and decisions that put me in the same less than human position as the African-Americans the *New York Times* was seeking to protect.

At present, libel law strips defamation victims of their right to life, liberty, and the pursuit of happiness. It fosters and condones cruel and unusual punishment. It is an embarrassment to the men and women who have worked diligently from the formation of this nation to make it a rare haven in the world where individual rights are not secondary to pursuit of wealth, power, and control.

It was the Supreme Court of the United States that created the problem -- and only the Supreme Court that can fix it. We all make mistakes, and it is time for you to fix this one.

May the pendulum swing back to the middle. May suppression of the media in reporting the truth never be condoned. May we return to a time when responsibility in reporting and human rights are of equal and high value.

* * * * *

God bless you all. May you have long, happy, and productive careers as members of the Supreme Court.

Watching The Wheels
(Original Epilogue)

"I'm just sitting here watching the wheels go round and round,
I really love to watch them turn,
No longer riding on the Merry-go-round,
I just had to let it go."

John Lennon, "Watching the Wheels"

"Faith in a holy cause is to a considerable extent a substitute for the lost faith in ourselves."

Eric Hoffer, <u>The True Believer</u>

"It ain't over till it's over."

Yogi Berra

On July 29, 1994 the Court of Appeals, Thirteenth Judicial District issued a judgment and opinion that partially remanded the Summary Judgment of the 152nd District Court -- ordering my case to trial.

The following letter outlines my thoughts on the matter. The justices of the Appellate Court clearly made an honest and appropriate decision given the information and law available to them -- but the partial rather than full remanding is the subject of my concern.

* * * * *

August 22, 1994

Mr. Wayne Paris
6363 Woodway
Suite 902
Houston, Texas 77057

Dear Wayne:

Thank you for the tremendous job in getting us headed back to trial! The enclosed selections from Professor Powe's book have always been on my mind -- and perhaps now they are the subject of some thinking by Hearst et al.

I do not have the money nor the inclination to argue with you about your recommendation to avoid appeal of the partial rather than full remanding of the district court summary judgment. However, it is important to me that you understand that this mistake on the part of the Court of Appeals is, in my mind, further proof of the sad state of libel law in this country. In the briefest summary possible my arguments are:

> The judges failed to consider the deposition of Catherine Chriss in which she specifically stated that she never believed that I was anti-woman, drug abusing, homosexual, or neo-Nazi. How is it that she can rely on something to be "substantially true" that she openly admits she <u>never</u> believed to be true?
>
> If they based their decision on my deposition in Wyatt *v. Sakowitz* how did they miss my one word response of "No" when asked under oath if I had been a member (as opposed to a recruit) of the cult?

Of all possible arguments the most pertinent may be that the picture painted of me on the front page of their paper is simply not true. This decision on the part of the court of appeals upholds the right of media in the United States to lie with no fear of consequence. As long as the courts uphold this misuse of Constitutional privilege our modern media will be a threat to the vitality and longevity of the nation.

Catherine Chriss breached a contract that she made, and I look forward to working with you to find out if Hearst really wants to let twelve of my peers decide which of us is telling the truth. Although they have proven themselves to be adept at lying I doubt if their lies will play well before those who do not depend upon them for fees or re-election.

Please let me know when discovery opens again. I have a great deal of interest in knowing what players in the chain of command at Hearst participated in the decision to move for summary judgment after their counsel was notified of criminal activity relevant to the suit. In that regard, we might do well to have a guest list for Cobra's recent gala. The local gossip columns talked about Mayor Lanier's attendance but did not include many names of the other three hundred in attendance. My guess is that the list would be revealing with regard to his influence on both the media and the judiciary.

Thank you again for a great job against overwhelming odds.

Sincerely,

Roger Hall

*****

The war continues rather than ends, but it is now a war over a broken promise rather than a lie. I will no doubt have to answer many unrelated questions over many fee driven hours as Hearst tries to avoid losing money -- rather than simply allowing a jury to decide who is telling the truth. Maybe by the time the trial starts I will have an interest in it.

For now I have bigger snakes to kill. It seems that child abuse is much more prevalent in my new home than could have been imagined so I am off to join the Guardian ad Litem program designed to monitor abused children and help them get the full value of their legal rights.

Lawyers and courts and substantial truth and rules for submission don't mean much to me anymore -- but somewhere out there is a kid who needs to learn how to survive in the snake pit long enough to become a Rockie. And I really need a third baseman who can handle a glove.

* * * * *

Someone else will have to bring you a case about libel.

I hope this story helps in some way when the time comes for you to make a decision on it.

Final Epilogue

In a mediation session in late 1995 the counsel for the Hearst Corporation told the mediator that they had not settled a libel suit since 1969.

* * * * *

The case of *Roger D. Hall v. The Hearst Corporation and Catherine Chriss* was settled out of court in December 1995.

KF 221 .L5 H35 1998

Date Due